"I adore Andi! Her unrestrained passion fo
lower is a compelling look at what it means
love of Jesus and unearth the beauty of ger
you to search your own relationship with (
walk the road less traveled.'"

Lisa Bevere, *New York Times* bestselling author and cofounder of Messenger International

"Andi has a powerful and urgent message for followers of Jesus. A hurting world is desperate to see the real thing, but the gospel must be real for us first. Are we living it or faking it? This book will challenge you and leave you equipped and encouraged to passionately follow Jesus in your sphere of influence. You were created to make a difference, and Andi will walk alongside you as you do."

Christine Caine, founder of Propel Women and A21

"Lisa's and my friend Andi knows what it means to passionately follow after Jesus. She speaks the truth in love and does not compromise it for popularity. In her new book, *Fake or Follower*, she challenges you to press into a deep and meaningful relationship with Jesus that will change you from the inside out!"

John Bevere, author and minister, Messenger International

"This book contains an important message. Do we have a real faith in Christ, or have we settled for a diluted look-alike? Real faith is worth fighting for, and Andi shows us how."

Sheila Walsh, cohost of Life Today and author of *It's Okay Not to Be Okay*

"Andi Andrew is a clarifying voice of compassion, coupled with truth, to a generation that is looking for answers about what life can truly be like with God. In her new book, *Fake or Follower*, she enlightens readers on the stark difference between living a passionate life that powerfully walks in the way of Jesus and living a fake imitation of it—hollow religion, rules, obligation, and mediocrity. If you're stuck in a loveless relationship with God governed by 'shoulds' and shame, confused about how to break free from a religious mindset, or longing for the 'more' you hope is possible with God, then this book is for you! Andi has a powerful gift of getting to the root of complex issues, and this book will help you connect to the love of God in the depths of your being, leaving you transformed and free!"

Kris Vallotton, leader, Bethel Church, Redding, CA; cofounder of Bethel School of Supernatural Ministry; and author of thirteen books, including *The Supernatural Ways of Royalty*, *Heavy Rain*, and *Poverty, Riches, and Wealth*

"Andi Andrew is an incredible leader! She's someone you want to hang around with because of her infectious love for all things real, applicable, and relevant to modern Christianity. She doesn't hold back in her new book, *Fake or Follower*.

Her writing is a perfect mixture of honesty and conviction. *Fake or Follower* will keep you asking serious questions about an honest and authentic walk with Christ. Everyone should read this book."

Havilah Cunnington, founder of Truth to Table
and author of *Stronger Than the Struggle*

"Andi Andrew is a gifted, captivating, witty, and brilliant communicator of God's Word; she brings it to life like no other. Our church and Arise Women's conferences have been greatly impacted by the transparency of her life and her Robin Williams–esque, genius back-and-forth-staccato style of communication. But as great a communicator as she is, her latest book, *Fake or Follower*, is the genuine article—a true literary work of authenticity that calls a generation of believers to live out our 'only message.' Andi's voice is heard through every sentence and her passion conveyed in every chapter. *Fake or Follower* has impacted our hearts, and if you allow it to, it will impact yours."

Mike and Lisa Kai, lead pastors, Inspire Church, Hawaii

"In a world focused on externals, appearances, and selfies, *Fake or Follower* is a breath of fresh air. With her trademark candor, honesty, passion, and humor, Andi Andrew reminds us that depth comes from depending on God each second of every day. I highly recommend this book for anyone longing to deepen their faith as they grow closer to Christ."

Chris Hodges, senior pastor, Church of the Highlands,
and author of *Fresh Air* and *The Daniel Dilemma*

"Over the years, I have been blessed to have a front-row seat to Andi's life. I can say without question that she is one of the most authentic people I have ever met. She is a prophet and a gifted leader whose love for Jesus is infectious. Her passion in life is to see people obtain freedom in Christ and to watch people flourish in their true callings. This book hits you directly in the heart while replenishing your soul. It will equip you to step further into your true identity in Christ."

Brian Harper, chief executive officer, Rouse Properties

"In a world suffocated with perfect poses and selfies, Andi challenges us to put away the filters and fight for authentic faith. *Fake or Follower* is poignant and powerful, and she boldly forced me to wrestle with my own faith and to question, Is my faith real or is this a show? Her book is humorous and engaging, and you will love how she makes diving deep into our faith so simple."

Bianca Juarez Olthoff, activist, Bible teacher, and
bestselling author of *Play with Fire*

"This is a must-read book in the midst of a generation that tries to appear perfect."

Heather Lindsey, author, speaker, and founder of Pinky Promise

"*Fake or Follower* has Pastor Andi's name written all over it—she lives this message of refusing to settle for a shallow faith. It is written with beautiful simplicity, and Pastor Andi is both inspirational and practical as she shares the life experiences that have led her to pen these amazing truths. Whether you are a new believer or have been on the journey awhile but have lost your way—knowing there is more but not knowing how to get there—you need to read this book. Within its pages you will discover fundamental truths on how to live a genuine, God-conscious, transformed life."

Jeff and Lorraine Wright, lead pastors, Green Pastures Church, Northern Ireland

"Anyone can go through the motions—faking it is easy. What's hard is living lives that matter, lives that have meaning beyond ourselves. That's what it means to follow Jesus, and that's why I'm excited for you to discover Andi's book and read about the incredible life God has for all of us who are sick and tired of fake."

Greg Surratt, founding pastor, Seacoast Church, and president of the Association of Related Churches

"It's all swirly these days. It's hard to tell what is genuine and what is just fanfare, noise, and nonsense. Enter Andi Andrew. Watch her face as she speaks and you will want to listen forever. You know that whatever she's dishing out is cut-you-to-the-core real. And the truth behind her words is not only eternity-minded but also life-shifting. I've had the joy of hearing her talk about Jesus in person, but I promise you reading her words in this book is not a consolation prize. Make a cup of coffee, pull up a chair, and feel the freedom to cut through the crazy and the clutter to hear some real words by a really wise woman. You're going to love this book, and it's going to change your life."

Jess Connolly, Bible teacher and author of *Wild and Free*, *Dance Stand Run*, and *Always Enough, Never Too Much*

"Our selfie society has rewarded fake while simultaneously destroying our witness, uniqueness, and true purpose. In this book, Andi challenges readers to move beyond the comfort of the mask and into a place of real commitment, where we live and lead with our God-given purpose at the center of everything."

Ronaldo Hardy, lead pastor, Love Alive Church

"Andi's passion pours out onto every page of this book. She casts a vision of faith that reaches beyond church attendance and spiritual well wishing and is instead a life-defining relationship with the living God. Then Andi takes us further, illustrating how following Jesus also transforms our relationships and compels us to engage deeply and authentically with the issues facing our communities and culture. Sharing biblical truths and vulnerable, personal stories, Andi inspires us to follow Jesus with our whole hearts and every area of our lives."

Jo Saxton, speaker, author of *The Dream of You*, and cohost of the *Lead Stories* podcast

"Christians are experiencing a crisis of credibility. Now as much as ever, the world is watching and wondering if we are who we say we are. That's why I am so grateful for the message of this book and the boldness of its call. Andi Andrew is inviting us into authentic, passionate, costly discipleship, and I think people are ready for it."

Sharon Hodde Miller, author of *Free of Me: Why Life Is Better When It's Not about You*

"There is a popular saying that goes, 'Fake it till you make it.' As an artist in the entertainment industry, I know all too well that this 'please-perform-perfect-never-enough' mentality runs rampant in pop culture, seeking to strip away identity and clip wings before people ever take flight. However, there is hope, and *Fake or Follower* serves as an awakener to that hope. It challenges the status quo of stopping at belief in the rules that come with religion, and it incites a hunger to step into an authentic relationship with Jesus. Only by responding to the daily invitation to follow Him do we become the people we were made to be. As Andi Andrew has written, 'Jesus came for a revolution inside our hearts that would transform our entire lives and, in turn, society.' Wherever you are in life, you don't have to fake it anymore. In fact, now is the time to refuse to fake it! Whether you have been a Christian for a lifetime or you have never set foot in a church, this book is for you. And don't just read and believe. Read and become."

Phillip Attmore, performance artist, writer, and speaker

"Andi is one of those funny, honest, and authentic people whom you always want to be around, and you'll feel that in her writing. *Fake or Follower* is filled with brilliant storytelling and insights that make you say, 'Wow, I needed that.' So don't pick up this book unless you're ready to keep reading! Get ready to be inspired."

Peter Haas, pastor, SubstanceChurch.com; author of humor books, *Pharisectomy* and *Broken Escalators*; and DJ producer for Substance Variant

"Through her experience in life and ministry, Andi is able to convey incredible spiritual insights in her book *Fake or Follower*. In a time when authenticity in our Christian lives is so vital for our world, the message in this book is much needed. We believe this book will become a great resource for many people."

Steve and Sharon Kelly, senior pastors, Wave Church

FAKE OR FOLLOWER

REFUSING TO SETTLE FOR A SHALLOW FAITH

ANDI ANDREW

BakerBooks
a division of Baker Publishing Group
Grand Rapids, Michigan

Published by Baker Books
a division of Baker Publishing Group
PO Box 6287, Grand Rapids, MI 49516-6287
www.bakerbooks.com

Printed in the United States of America

Library of Congress Cataloging-in-Publication Data
Names: Andrew, Andi, 1978– author.
Title: Fake or follower : refusing to settle for a shallow faith / Andi Andrew.
Description: Grand Rapids : Baker Publishing Group, 2018. | Includes bibliographical references.
Identifiers: LCCN 2018014414 | ISBN 9780801093296 (pbk.)
Subjects: LCSH: Christian women—Religious life.
Classification: LCC BV4527 .A529 2017 | DDC 248.8/43—dc23
LC record available at https://lccn.loc.gov/2018014414

Author is represented by The Christopher Ferebee Agency, www.christopherferebee.com

18 19 20 21 22 23 24 7 6 5 4 3 2 1

My prayer is that when I die, all of hell rejoices
that I am out of the fight.

C. T. Studd

For Jenny, my mum-in-love

You fought the good fight. You finished the race. You kept the faith.

You followed Jesus with everything and left behind a stunningly beautiful legacy.

You refused to stay in the shallows but waded into the depths of His great love.

Back here on earth, we miss you and yet are so grateful that we have forever.

To my four world changers—Zeke, Jesse, Finley, and Sammy

This is a love letter for you.

xoxo

Contents

Introduction

Being confronted with death has a way of causing us to take a look at our lives and ask the question, "What *really* matters?"

The diagnosis tore us apart: an inoperable brain tumor. A ticking time bomb, barring a Hail Mary miracle, was growing in the beautiful mind of the woman I called Mum, my Australian-born husband's mother, Jenny. She was young and beautiful and, as an accomplished pianist, just beginning to compose some of the most stunning, heaven-breathed music. She spoke an eternal language through her fingers and into our hearts. Even in her last days, when she could no longer speak, we'd put on her music, and she'd cock her head sideways, registering with the language that had always made sense to her—music.

On November 17, 2017, she left this planet and walked into the arms of her Savior. Selfishly, I felt robbed. Robbed of all the years ahead that *I* wanted her to be a part of—my children graduating, getting married, having *her* great-grandchildren so that she could hold them in her arms and bless them with innumerable kisses. And I wanted her for *me* too, not just for my kids. We had worked so hard at our relationship. It was tender, real, connected, honest, and beautiful, but not without a fight. She truly had become my mum, and just like that, the breath in her lungs was gone.

In the middle of a yearlong battle that our family walked through together, I was beginning to write this very book you hold in your hands. The way she lived her life got me deeply pondering my own. Inspiration for the words you're about to read came with a somewhat morbid thought: *If I were to die in a year's time, what letter would I want to write to my children, the church, and the generations to come? What would I want to leave with them?*

As quickly as I had the thought, the answer came to me—I would want them to know the difference between a life lived faking it with a hollow religion, obligation, mediocrity, people pleasing, and rule following and a life lived passionately following Jesus. A life lived drawing a line in the sand, committing to a beautiful journey of discovery on the road less traveled, full of revelation, mistakes, and honest moments; relationships lived in reciprocity, simplicity, and power. A life lived discovering how to powerfully walk in the ways of Jesus on a daily basis, learning and adhering to the truth and stepping into the life that Jesus died to give them, seeing His kingdom come and His will be done here on earth as it is in heaven. Following Jesus is a daily invitation for more, and it's not always easy. This is how Jenny, my mum-in-law, followed Jesus, and it was beautiful to behold.

In our padded, materialistic, overstimulated Western society, Christianity has become more of a "rote religion"—a list of things you should and shouldn't do, devoid of a relationship with the One who loves you the most—than a passionate relationship with the living God manifest by internal and cultural transformation. I believe there is a generation alive today shaken with a holy discomfort of simply going through the motions. In response, they are crying out to know what following in the ways of Jesus really means for our everyday lives. I believe many are willing to fit the bill; we need not dumb down the price tag.

Jesus came for a revolution inside our hearts that would transform our entire lives and, in turn, society. The more we know Him, the more we discover our true identity and our destiny here on earth; the two go hand in hand. Following Jesus is about the pursuit of His heart and a deeper understanding of the gospel and how the Good News is worked out in our lives and the lives of those around us.

Gospel means "good news," which indicates there was bad news to start with that Jesus came to reverse. Jesus's life, death, and resurrection are both timely and timeless. There is no other gospel but death and resurrection. First Jesus's death and resurrection and then our own as we are crucified with Christ *and* resurrected in *His* life as a new creation. Jesus said:

> And anyone who comes to me must be willing to share my cross and experience it as his own, or he cannot be considered to be my disciple. So don't follow me without considering what it will cost you. For who would construct a house before first sitting down to estimate the cost to complete it? Otherwise he may lay the foundation and not be able to finish. (Luke 14:27–29 TPT)

Let us consider the cost and then willingly pay the price as we follow Jesus, daily becoming more like Him. May we run our race with perseverance and passion until the day of completion.

Friends, Christ is my *only* message. It is my passion to ignite and awaken hearts all around the world to His goodness and love. My hope is that you will stop settling and welcome the discomfort of what it looks like to truly follow Jesus on a daily basis, allowing the wise Teacher to sculpt you until you breathe your last breath. My prayer is that you will step out of the shallows and into the deep with Him. Colossians 1:28–29 is a life verse for me:

> Christ is our message! We preach to awaken hearts and bring every person into the full understanding of truth. It has become my inspiration and passion in ministry to labor with a tireless intensity, with his power flowing through me, to present to every believer the revelation of being his perfect one in Jesus Christ. (TPT)

The truth is we are all imperfect people walking in His perfect love. We are pilgrims on a journey, discovering new things every day, learning in the moments life brings while being transformed as we go. With that premise, I humbly present to you in the pages of this book a snippet of the personal revelation I have attempted to walk in during my twenty years of following Jesus.

We'll touch on the entertainment culture, salvation, and the profound invitation to follow Jesus, who embodies the way, the truth, and the life we are to live. We'll look at the reality of living out the Sermon on the Mount, what true love really is, the identity crises we face, and our misplaced worship in today's society. We'll talk about God's healing and transformation taking place in community, not isolation, while holding in tension the need for purposeful solitude in a world that's overstimulating and demanding. We'll talk about discipleship, "a long obedience in the same direction" over a lifetime.[1] We'll discuss the Western cultural captivity of the church and whether we're posting a life mantra on social media or actually living it out in our daily lives. And, of course, we'll talk about others—we're free to set others free; we are reconciled reconcilers. This is not a self-help gospel; it is good news for all.

As you read these pages, may you dig deep, weigh every word, and bring them before God. Agree or disagree, but whatever you do, always let it point you back to the Father because Jesus made a way to His heart and gave us the Word of God and the gift of the Holy Spirit to remind us of all truth. Keep putting one foot in front of the other, living this beautiful, messy, intricate tapestry of a life, following Jesus one day at a time, and humbly learning as you go. You'll make mistakes and blunders; you'll get hurt and you'll hurt some people along the way too. But don't lose hope or heart, and never give up. There is so much more to discover. Please, just don't fake it, because a genuine life before God is worth the cost. May you boldly continue to walk along the road less traveled.

My mother-in-law's life was a *lived* love letter to the church, and this book is my love letter to you.

Jenny followed Jesus with everything she had, from the moment she gave her life to Him until the moment she breathed her last and walked into her Savior's arms. The music she composed will echo into eternity and our hearts forever and so will the trail she blazed for generations to come. Her life has left a passionate legacy of following Jesus with complete abandon. She has made an eternal imprint on our hearts.

May this book awaken you to the breath you *still* have in your lungs so that you don't waste a single one.

1

Refuse to Fake It

> A disciple will be repaid for what he has learned and followed, for God pays no attention to the titles or prestige of men.
>
> Colossians 3:25 TPT

She said I was "cute and entertaining." Cute and *en-ter-tain-ing*. Take me now, Lord.

I had just finished speaking at a church, having completely poured myself out and at my most vulnerable, when a well-meaning woman said I was cute and entertaining. I'm sure she thought it was a compliment, but she may as well have slapped me across the face, and I didn't feel like turning the other cheek. My internal dialogue went into an unholy nosedive.

Her words may have had more to do with what she came to the gathering to receive than what I was actually giving, but they hit me hard, and so they should have. Instantly, I went into a contemplative, internal spiral. If thoughts could be heard, mine would have sounded like deep, guttural cries for God to search my heart: *Am I really only cute and entertaining? Is that all I have to give? Is that what I've been doing all this time, feeding consumers with entertainment? If so, then what is the point? God, if that's the case, forgive me . . . oh, and also, I quit.*

A tad dramatic, but that's truly how I felt in the moment. God has given me the gift of humor when I communicate, and it often comes out right before I bring a truth in love that's potentially hard to hear. Laughter has a way of softening the heart to hear what God desires to say. But upon hearing her "compliment," I had to ask myself a hard question: *Am I entertaining people, or am I teaching and, more importantly, living in the fullness of the gospel?* Humanity is desperate for the good news that we are restored in Jesus to our redemptive and created purpose in the middle of a world full of pain and suffering. All eyes are on the church to see if we're really living out what we say we believe. Again, I had to ask myself, *Am I following Jesus and leading others in the way to follow Him, or am I faking it, putting on a show and aiding in implementing Western consumerist culture in the church?*

The last thing I want to do is be fake or put on a show—ever.

Think about this: every painter's work is imperfect, but even the imperfections of a master craftsman can make their work incredibly valuable. But a fake is worth almost nothing. In fact, in most industries, producing fakes is a crime. A fake *isn't* what it's pretending to be. The seller of a fake is hoping you'll be fooled and pay full price for something that is only a cheap imitation. Fakes rip people off. And the one who "sells" us a watered-down, fake, impotent Christianity is the enemy of our souls. As followers of Jesus, we should have endless grace for imperfections but zero tolerance for fakes. Sometimes we are simply more influenced by modern culture, accepting it as our highest form of reality and allowing it to become our ecosystem rather than creating a heavenly culture and ecosystem here on earth.

It took me a while to unwind that evening, but once I calmed down, I dozed off and entered a vivid dream state. The first place I found myself was in downtown Brooklyn, close to where I live, with my two youngest children, Finley and Sammy. My guardian angel was also with me and at my right shoulder the entire time. We were peaceful and safe, but the scene around us was far from either. I looked over to the subway entrance and saw a crowd gathered, taking pictures and videos with their phones of people who had been executed and piled on top of each other the night before. Policemen were trying to move the people on, but they were making a spectacle of death, exploiting others' pain and tragedy in broad daylight. As I turned into the square and walked past Borough Hall, severed heads charred by fire were everywhere. I looked down and realized that land mines had been set throughout the streets and the square to take out unsuspecting citizens. I knew in my gut that we were surveying the damage from a raid that had occurred the night before—the enemy was on the prowl, destroying lives, and I had brought my children with me to open their eyes to the realities of the world they were living in and called to love. I had no desire to hide them from it. With a confident nod of assurance from my angel, I walked hand in hand with my children right into the minefield without any fear.

In the next scene of the dream, we found ourselves underground in a secret passageway that led to safety. We all had total peace in the midst of chaos as we walked home, picking up supplies from the stark shelves of the underground convenience store for the journey. Before I knew it, the scene switched again. All four of my kids, my husband, my mom and dad, and I were sleeping together in a room in an apartment building on the eighth floor in Crown Heights. I knew another murderous raid was about to take place, so I went to the window to keep watch. A mob was gathering on the street, lighting bombs and running into the building where we were sleeping. I quickly stirred everyone, and we hastily escaped.

I woke up from the dream disturbed and shaken, asking God if it was a nightmare or if it had any meaning. As I processed with the Holy Spirit, I began to understand that the dream represented the times we're living in. The enemy is setting traps and land mines for unsuspecting citizens roaming the earth, while at the same time humanity makes a spectacle of death via news channels and social media, exploiting the pain and trauma of the vulnerable. Sometimes this even happens in the church. If we could simply put our phones down more often and intentionally be about our Father's business—unfolding before our eyes—we'd see the change and transformation we long for that we post about on our feeds.

Taking my children by the hand into the chaos showed me that we aren't to shield them from the pain we see in this world but to show them how the gospel fills the gaps. I was reminded that we don't live out this life for ourselves only. We are charged with the mission to intentionally raise up the next generation, walking hand in hand into the middle of a broken world and passionately living out the good news of His great love and salvation together.

Being underground in the dream represented the truth that He has granted every life safe passage home, but there are still so many who need to know the way to go. We have the ability to open the door and show them the way (2 Cor. 5:18–20). Being in the apartment on the eighth floor in Crown Heights with family symbolized our new beginning (represented by the number eight) with Christ, crowned (Crown Heights) as sons and daughters of the king, living life together in family and community while watching and praying over one another (Matt. 26:41). We do this so that when attacks and invasions take place in our lives, we have one another to help us shoulder the burden and get through. Life is a battlefield full of land mines, both seen and unseen. It's important that we have friends and loved ones to keep watch when we are anxious, weary, and in the middle of a fight. As followers of Jesus, we can walk right into the middle of it all with confident assurance, and our lives can show others how to walk into the fray without fear. Following Jesus isn't safe. It's an adventure that will take us to places inside ourselves and outside ourselves in this beautiful, messy world that He loves so deeply, but only if we're willing to go. I love what Mr. Beaver says of Aslan in *The Lion, the Witch and the*

Wardrobe: "'Course he isn't safe. But he's good. He's the King, I tell you."[1]

I think we can all agree that the last thing a lost and dying world needs is an army of cute entertainers who are only interested in putting on a show with an impotent gospel that temporarily fixes our symptoms but doesn't heal the heart, soul, and body. Faking it is not how we intend to live, and sometimes, when we do find ourselves doing so, even unintentionally, we're not really sure how we got there. We *all need* the reality of Jesus, not just a religious concept of who He is. And we need to see the manifestation of the good news He brings in and through our lives in the midst of the darkness, where bad things are still happening to good people on a daily basis. To be clear, God does not cause bad things to happen; He is good to the core and has only goodness to give. We live in a fallen world that is in grave need of the good news of the gospel through Jesus Christ who reconciles all things. We are empowered to pray that His kingdom come and His will be done here on earth as it is in heaven (Matt. 6:10) to thwart the darkness and cancel every assignment of the enemy, releasing God's goodness wherever we go.

My husband, Paul, has often spoken of the time he gave his life to Jesus at age sixteen. His passion for Jesus and the house of God became so extreme that his parents, who weren't believers at the time, thought he had joined a cult. He had become a new person, turning from the life he once lived and choosing to walk with passion in a completely different direction, following Jesus with his entire life. His internal world was leading his external world. Before this, Paul had gone to Catholic school and to church for Easter and Christmas each year with his family to be, in his words, "inoculated with just enough Christianity not to take it too seriously." I think somehow in our Western, consumerist culture, the Good News has been lost on some of us—maybe because we've mixed in just a little bit of Jesus, inoculating ourselves with Him rather than gladly surrendering our whole lives.

In some ways, we've relegated the Christian life to a moment of conversion, a lifting of our hand in a service with eyes closed and head bowed, when this moment is only the beginning of a beautiful, deep, and wide adventure full of twists and turns. Instead, after our moment of turning from our ways and turning to God, we often become consumers of the Christian life on our own terms. We look for a church that meets our needs and attend as regularly as possible, but if that church stops meeting our needs or offends us, we go and find another one, sometimes as easily as we buy a new pair of shoes. We've got to ask ourselves, *Since when did the church become all about us?*

There are social structures, systemic injustices, and corporate sins of the nations we are a part of that are in need of the transformation only the kingdom of heaven can bring. But as long as we are simply looking to be fed, entertained, and have only *our* needs met, the corporate needs of our communities go unnoticed, ignored, and neglected. True community is messy, but it is where sanctification, revelation, confrontation, activation, and transformation take place. When we try to follow Jesus on our own because "I'm the church and don't need to go to church to be a part of it," we miss out on the fullness of being part of a body—we miss out on becoming more like Christ as we rub shoulders with imperfect people who give us the opportunity to repent, forgive, and grow. Just as severed toes and limbs are useless and dead to the body, I'd go so far as to say that *so are we* when we run away from what we became a part of the moment we surrendered our lives to Jesus.

Following Jesus is a long game, an adventure that requires us to lay down our lives and follow Him daily but not out of a loveless obedience. We follow Him out of a knowing that we are so loved that our lives were worth dying for. As a result, we are saved and reconciled back to our created purpose, and then we willingly lay down our lives for others. When the good news of the gospel becomes a genuine reality for us, we stop faking it through religious obligation and begin to lovingly and passionately follow Jesus anywhere, anytime—no matter the cost. Friends, just imagine your guardian angel giving you a nod of assurance to step right into all that God has for you—without any fear.

I Could Sing of Your Love Forever

Spokane Christian Center, July 31, 1998, are the place and day I fell in love. I was literally blindsided by God's pure, extravagant, overwhelming love in the most beautiful way. Growing up with parents who were imperfect and flawed but deeply loving reflected something of the heart of God, so when I encountered His heart so clearly for the first time, I clung to it with desperate passion. My moment of conversion was radical, real, and raw. I had no desire to go back to my old life after experiencing that kind of love and acceptance. That moment on a summer evening was as real as they come.

It had been a roller coaster of a year for nineteen-year-old me. I was in the midst of a big breakup and near the end of my first year of college at the University of Washington when it came to a crashing finish when my best friend's mom passed away during finals week. I woke up crying one morning with a gut feeling that something was wrong. I called my mom only to hear her crying and telling me that Janet's time was near. Janet wasn't just a friend of my mom's; she was like a second mother to me. Her daughter Brittani and I played together our entire upbringing and went to high school together. She was my best friend and is still like a sister to this day.

I ran across campus to the house of my older sister, Kristin, in my pajamas to tell her Janet was dying and I needed to get to Brittani to be with her. My shoulders were heaving as I ran sobbing through the quad. This was before cell phones, and my sister wasn't picking up her landline. When I got there, she held me for a moment and then went into big-sister mode, got on the phone, and bought me a plane ticket home. Hours later I was in the plane, but Janet left her earthly home while I was in the air.

Broken that I didn't have a chance to say good-bye, I needed closure. The next day I walked alone into the room where she lay at the funeral home to view the open casket. Upon seeing her face, I gasped and covered my mouth, quietly sobbing. She was gone. Her body was there, but her spirit, the essence of Janet, was not. Something deep ricocheted into my heart—eternal life is real; our bodies are an earthly home that will one day pass away. I wasn't following Jesus at the time, but I was so close. That moment drew me nearer to the truth.

That summer I traveled around the United States as a professional cheerleader and taught at summer camps for teenagers. This tour was my last crazy hurrah in search of love before I came face-to-face with the real thing. Arriving home after the end of my tour, I went with my parents to the night meeting of the summer camp at their new church. We arrived late, the lights were down, and the chorus of a song by Delirious? was being sung over and over again: "I could sing of your love forever."[2] And just like that, I hit a wall of love that melted into what felt like liquid, enveloping every inch of my body and seeping into hidden crevices of deep brokenness from prior years of suppressed pain. I was done for—in all the best ways.

When the evangelist for the evening spoke about what following Jesus means, it took everything in me to stay in my seat. My body was physically buzzing with this new infiltration of love, as if every cell in my body were vibrating, transforming my DNA into love. I wanted to shout at the top of my lungs to everyone in the room what was happening inside me. When the speaker asked who wanted to give their life to Jesus, we were encouraged to lift our hands. Instead, I shot to my feet and ran to the front—I didn't have time for this "hand raising" business—because all I wanted to do was crash tackle Jesus with everything in me. I was done with my way; it wasn't working. I was completely undone and in love. As I stood there in front of God and everyone, I whispered under my breath to the God of heaven who had come into my heart, "This is all I want to do—I just want to build Your church." I had no idea what I was really saying or where that desire would take me, but all these years later I am still on the greatest adventure with the One who is always near, faithful, kind, and true.

That night I went home and cracked open the Bible my dad and mom had given me for my eighteenth birthday in hopes that I'd read it. I hadn't really until that night, and the pages just "happened" to open to this passage:

> "Come now, let us settle the matter,"
>   says the Lord.
> "Though your sins are like scarlet,
>   they shall be as white as snow;
> though they are red as crimson,
>   they shall be like wool." (Isa. 1:18)

Weeping with joy and gratitude, I was still overcome with a visceral response to this extravagant grace and love, welcoming them with open arms. Jesus and His great love for me settled the matter. I was clean, new, and restored to my created purpose as a reflector of God's image on earth. For the first time in a very long time, I felt like me.

The Problem and the Solution

Why do we begin to fake it after we find, and are found by, such honest and real love? I believe the problem is that we live in a world filled with a lot of bad news, obsessed with self, and consumed with the need for more. At times it may even feel like the world is falling apart as we're confronted daily with racism, classism, sexism, suicide, anxiety and depression, and the collapse of the family unit. Not to mention shootings, the refugee crisis, mass incarceration, sex and labor trafficking, a nation divided, the threat of world war, and Christians being beheaded and killed in various nations. Even the church, which is created to be one body, has been tearing itself apart with prideful arrogance, all in the name of being right as though we've found some corner on God no one else knows about. So we stand on our soapboxes and simultaneously mutilate the body of Christ we are meant to be one with.

I am a local church girl who believes that a healthy, thriving, imperfect, honest community of people who continue to grapple with the depths of the gospel and their created value *can absolutely* change the world one person at a time—together. I pray that we would continually be challenged individually and corporately by the reality of the gospel in our lives.

One of the hurdles we face within the Western church in regard to the gospel is twofold: either we believe in a gospel we can attain with our bare hands and then maintain with rules, or we operate in a comfort-driven gospel in which we are told, "If you've had a hard year or a tough life, come close to God today (as if He is far away) and He will make your life better." When we walk out of the four walls of the church into the places we're divinely positioned to *be* the church and make a difference, we can feel ill equipped to do so.

The antidote to the problem is that we have *the* Good News! Really good news—the kind that is full of God's goodness, mercy, grace, and power—literally turning our lives upside down. And more than just having good news, it's imperative that we see it working in our lives and, in turn, our spheres of influence. We can get so focused on the world around us that we forget Jesus came to set our hearts free within us to release the kingdom of heaven outside us. He didn't come to deal merely with the symptoms of humanity but to fix the root of the problem. He came for not only our hearts but also our entire lives.

We Must Be Born Again

The term *born again* has lost some of its deep meaning in our day and age, but it's not just Christianese. Let's break it down because at its core is the solution to the bad news we're surrounded with. That we can be born again *is* good news.

> Now there was a Pharisee, a man named Nicodemus who was a member of the Jewish ruling council. He came to Jesus at night and said, "Rabbi, *we* know that you are a teacher who has come from God. For no one could perform the signs you are doing if God were not with him."
>
> Jesus replied, "Very truly I tell you, no one can see the kingdom of God unless they are *born again*."
>
> "How can someone be born when they are old?" Nicodemus asked. "Surely they cannot enter a second time into their mother's womb to be born!"
>
> Jesus answered, "Very truly I tell you, no one can enter the kingdom of God unless they are *born of water and the Spirit*. Flesh gives birth to flesh, but the Spirit gives birth to spirit. You should not be surprised at my saying, 'You must be born again.' The wind blows wherever it pleases. You hear its sound, but you cannot tell where it comes from or where it is going. So it is with everyone born of the Spirit."
>
> "How can this be?" Nicodemus asked. (John 3:1–9, emphasis added)

Such a good question; let's explore this further. First of all, Nicodemus said, "*We* know that you are a teacher who has come from God." Nicodemus was part of the Jewish ruling council, those who were in charge of keeping watch over the letter of the law, and Jesus was messing with their theology. It was a compliment that Nicodemus called Him a teacher, but he came under the cover of night, in hiding, to ask Jesus his questions on behalf of the Jewish ruling council. They knew Jesus had come from God because there was no way that on His own He could perform the signs, wonders, and miracles they were seeing. I wonder if Nicodemus had any inkling that this was the Messiah, the One who would turn the tide and save God's people from toil, animal sacrifice, and self-preservation once and for all.

I can only imagine that Nicodemus must have been pondering in his heart why we needed to be "born again." The answer is found in the very beginning: the creation and fall of man as described in Genesis. God formed man from the dirt and breathed His image, "the breath of life" (2:7), into us for a purpose: to reproduce His image and fill the earth with His glory (1:28). When Adam and Eve were deceived into eating from the tree of the knowledge of good and evil by Satan, which God promised would surely kill them (2:17), the first result described was that "they realized they were naked" (3:7). Just one chapter earlier, the Bible noted that "Adam and his wife were both naked, and they felt no shame" (2:25). But the fruit of spiritual death was self-consciousness—a turning to self rather than to God. From the time of Adam and Eve's sin, mankind has been born into the sin of Adam, forced to toil for protection and provision, no longer preoccupied with reproducing God's image through love and relationship but instead seeking for themselves. The *Good News* is that Jesus, the second Adam, came to reconcile us back to our Father and redeem all that was lost in the garden.

When Jesus referred to being born of water *and* the Spirit, it was in response to Nicodemus raising the question of natural, physical birth and the impossibility of us going back into our mother's womb. It is as if Jesus was correcting Nicodemus by saying, "No, Nicodemus, you must be born both naturally and spiritually." In natural birth, before the baby enters the world, the amniotic sac bursts (hence, "my water broke"), and thus we are born of water. Think about the deep meaning of baptism in the context of being born again. First Peter 3:21 says, "This water symbolizes baptism that now saves you also—not the removal of dirt from the body but the pledge of a clear conscience toward God. It saves you by the resurrection of Jesus Christ." And Colossians 2:12 says, "Having been buried with him in baptism, in which you were also raised with him through your faith in the working of God, who raised him from the dead." Being baptized in water after we are born again of the Spirit declares to the world that our old life has died and we are now resurrected and made new in Christ's life.

To be born of the Spirit means we acknowledge that God is our Creator and Lord. We then purposefully turn from toiling and self-preservation to reconnect to the One who put our very breath and spirit within us while we were being knit together in our mother's womb (Ps. 139:13). When we acknowledge Jesus as our Lord, Savior, and Redeemer, who came to earth to ransom our lives *so that* we could be born again of the Spirit, we start to find ourselves living God-conscious lives, walking in the fullness of our created purpose and identity. Jesus said in John 14:6: "I am the *way*, and the *truth*, and the *life*; no one comes to the Father but through Me" (NASB, emphasis added). Acknowledging the Son is the way to the heart of the Father. In His arms we are born again, recognizing that He is our Father and we are His sons and daughters.

God doesn't hate the world and didn't come to punish it; God so *loves* the world that He sent His Son Jesus to redeem it back to Himself, and we, as Christ followers, are part of that redemption plan! We *get* to open the door to love!

> For God so loved the world that he gave his one and only Son, that whoever believes in him shall not perish but have eternal life. For God did not send his Son into the world to condemn the world, but to save the world through him. Whoever believes in him is not condemned, but whoever does not believe stands condemned already because they have not believed in the name of God's one and only Son. This is the verdict: Light has come into the world, but people loved darkness instead of light because their deeds were evil. Everyone who does evil hates the light, and will not come into the light for fear that their deeds will be exposed. But whoever lives by the truth comes into the light, so that it may be seen plainly that what they have done has been done in the sight of God. (John 3:16–21)

Truly following Jesus means that we surrender to the light of His great love and allow our deeds and heart motives to be exposed so that we begin to live true and honest lives that are God-conscious, not self-conscious. We long to reflect the glory and image of God on earth because after we understand how good this news is, we can't keep it to ourselves!

Maybe we keep the rules to stay in the good books because we've encountered a rote religion or we're indoctrinated with a fear of going to hell instead of encountering the radical love that *has* rescued us from hell. This is the kind of love that transforms a life and calls us into relationship—not obligation. It's the kind of love that causes us to jump all in without fear of rejection. My hope is that throughout this book you will continually encounter the true nature of God, compelling you to walk in your created purpose. My prayer is that we'll all stop only consuming and start giving too.

The Way, the Truth, and the Life

After processing my wild dream, I began to ask myself if I was a *fake* or a *follower.* Was I leading others to be fake and go through the motions, or was I living and showing the way to be a follower of Jesus, walking in the fullness of the gospel's transforming love?

As this question took up residence in my thought life, it led to a journey of uncovering what I have found throughout my twenty-year love story with God, of discovering what it means to be a follower of Jesus. I have many more years of life within me and still so much to learn, but just as the apostle Paul wrote passionate letters to the churches all over the earth in his time, so this is my love letter to the church today. It's a love letter about the difference between a life lived faking it with a hollow religion, mindless obligation, fear of man, and rule following and a life lived passionately loved and in love, following Jesus. A life lived drawing a line in the sand, committing to a beautiful journey of discovery and adventure, full of revelation, raw authenticity, honest emotion, mistakes made and learned from, repentance, forgiveness, reconciliation, and relationships lived in reciprocity. A life marked by zeal, simplicity, power, and most of all love. A life lived as our true selves, reflecting the image of God here on earth.

The question we should all ask ourselves on a regular basis is, *Am I faking it, or am I following Jesus?* I write this to you as a daughter, wife, mother, pastor, leader, and friend. As a woman who is learning more and more each day that life is finite and our pilgrimage on earth is practice for our eternal life in heaven.

It is such good news that Jesus didn't come so we could put on a show, living from the outside in, appeasing our guilty conscience by checking the box of Sunday church attendance. It's good news that we don't have to join the ranks of consumer Christians, living impotent lives Monday through Saturday. It's good news that He came so we may know the way to live, the truth to walk in, and the life we have no matter what we face. Jesus said, "I am the way and the truth and the life. No one comes to the Father except through me" (John 14:6).

Jesus is the embodiment of the *way* to the heart of the Father as we live a life reconciled to love. He shows us the way to live by personifying the method, because Jesus is the method. Self-help books and worldly methods can only take us so far. Watchman Nee said, "If all we get is merely a method, we will soon discover its ineffectiveness. God has not given us a method; He gives His own Son to us."[3] The more we know the Son, the more we know the way in which we are designed to live.

There are many facets to Christ's nature. He is full of fire and passion and is also the Prince of Peace. He operated in righteous anger, flipping over tables in the temple, and He celebrated at a wedding, turning water into wine. He is confrontational and at times mysterious, leaving us scratching our heads in wonder. He encouraged Peter in his revelation and rebuked him in the same breath for getting in the way. He led his disciples and taught them in very personal, immersive ways and sent them out before they were probably "ready." He came against the religious leaders and showed everyone a new way, the way of the kingdom, by performing signs, wonders, and miracles, manifesting the ministry of reconciliation. He sat at meals with wealthy sinners and rescued the outcast, poor, and downtrodden. He healed the multitudes and spent time alone with His Father in solitude. He is the Lion and the Lamb, and He cannot be tamed.

If we can continue to humbly learn what it means to follow in the *way* for the rest of our lives, embracing mystery and being committed to discovery, we'll stay on our knees and in love. This is not only for a lifetime but also for eternity.

Jesus is the *truth* we are longing to hear, see, taste, touch, and deeply know in a world full of lies and half-truths in which everyone has their own fluid "truth." Before Jesus was crucified, Pilate looked Him in the eyes and asked Him, "What is truth?" (John 18:38), unaware that truth incarnate, the bedrock and cornerstone, was standing right before him. The more we get to know Jesus and follow His ways, the more we understand truth because truth is a person. Truth is not merely a doctrine we uphold; it's the person Jesus whom we follow and know intimately. He is the truth that we are invited to know more deeply each day and that has the power to set us free.

Jesus is the *life* we are all genuinely longing to live enveloped in the midst of mundane, ordinary days; in the highlights and big events; and even in the darkness, trials, pain, and suffering we all face in different seasons. He is our true north—the eternity that has been placed in every heart trying to find home (Eccles. 3:11). For Christ, being and bringing life was effortless, because it's not just what He does but who He is. How often we toil to truly live by doing what we believe to be the right thing according to the expectations of others or even the unreasonable expectations of ourselves and in the end it feels lifeless and dead—when Jesus embodies the fullness of resurrection life that can infiltrate our every day. And we have access to *all* of Him!

The Invitation

We are invited to leave our old ways of thinking and living, selfish ambitions, preconceived ideas, religious systems, agendas, biases, and sometimes even the ways of our family of origin to learn that we're created anew and adopted into the family of God. This is profound in every way and requires our entire self, not just our big toe. Sometimes we wonder why transformation isn't taking place in our lives. Maybe it's because we're not following Jesus at all. Maybe we're following our own way with a little bit of Jesus mixed in. Maybe we've begun to fake it.

After Jesus spent forty days in the wilderness, he began to preach: "Repent, for the kingdom of heaven has come near" (Matt. 4:17). The Passion Translation says, "Keep turning away from your sins and come back to God, for heaven's kingdom realm is now accessible." To repent means to be sorry and change your ways. It's frustrating when my kids (or someone else) say they are sorry but keep doing the same thing. I frustrate myself when I do that! Are we living like this with God, desiring all the benefits of relationship with Him without action on our end? Throughout Jesus's three years of ministry on earth, He went everywhere telling people to repent (be sorry) and change their ways because the kingdom of heaven had come near! When we encounter His love and nature, we can't help but turn from self and look to Him for a new way to live.

In one of Jesus's many parables, He speaks of watchfulness, urgency, and readiness.

> Be dressed ready for service and keep your lamps burning, like servants waiting for their master to return from a wedding banquet, so that when he comes and knocks they can immediately open the door for him. It will be good for those servants whose master finds them watching when he comes. Truly I tell you, he will dress himself to serve, will have them recline at the table and will come and wait on them. It will be good for those servants whose master finds them ready, even if he comes in the middle of the night or toward daybreak. But understand this: If the owner of the house had known at what hour the thief was coming, he would not have let his house be broken into. You also must be ready, because the Son of Man will come at an hour when you do not expect him. (Luke 12:35–40)

When Jesus called the first disciples, they *immediately* left everything behind for an unknown adventure. They sensed the urgency of the hour and didn't waste their opportunity. Do you sense the urgency of the hour we now live in? Do you sense an urgency to follow Jesus anywhere, anytime with all that you are?

> As Jesus was walking beside the Sea of Galilee, he saw two brothers, Simon called Peter and his brother Andrew. They were casting a net into the lake, for they were fishermen. "Come, follow me," Jesus said, "and I will send you out to fish for people." At once they left their nets and followed him. Going on from there, he saw two other brothers, James

> son of Zebedee and his brother John. They were in a boat with their father Zebedee, preparing their nets. Jesus called them, and *immediately* they left the boat and their father and followed him. (Matt. 4:18–22, emphasis added)

Jesus addressed Simon Peter and Andrew's current life, a life of fishing, and then told them what they would become if they followed Him—and that was enough for them to literally leave everything behind. The invitation was clear, and so was their yes. He did it again with James and John. He simply called them and "immediately they left the *boat* and their *father* and followed him" (Matt. 4:22, emphasis added). They left their boat—their livelihood—for a promise of what? And they left their father, their family of origin, for an unknown journey. There is something about encountering Jesus that compels us to change everything because He is the life we are actually longing for. I pray that throughout these pages you'll encounter a living God who is worth the immediacy and urgency of living a life of true repentance, purpose, and all-out love.

To leave our old lives and follow Jesus is the opposite of transactional or religious living—it's transformational. Our lives begin to look different as we follow Him.

Is He truly our Lord *and* Savior, or are we treating Jesus as merely a good teacher whose words we can take or leave? C. S. Lewis puts it brilliantly:

> I am trying here to prevent anyone saying the really foolish thing that people often say about Him: I'm ready to accept Jesus as a great moral teacher, but I don't accept his claim to be God. That is the one thing we must not say. A man who was merely a man and said the sort of things Jesus said would

> not be a great moral teacher. He would either be a lunatic . . . or else he would be the Devil of Hell. You must make your choice. Either this man was, and is, the Son of God, or else a madman or something worse. You can shut him up for a fool, you can spit at him and kill him as a demon or you can fall at his feet and call him Lord and God, but let us not come with any patronizing nonsense about his being a great human teacher. He has not left that open to us. He did not intend to.[4]

I left my figurative boat on July 31, 1998—*not* to follow a lunatic but to follow the Son of God, Jesus, my Savior and newfound friend, on an adventure that has led me down roads I've loved, savored, loathed, sometimes resented, skipped down with joy, and questioned the validity of, but nonetheless I've embraced them with every fiber of my being. I have made my choice, as we all must.

So here is my invitation to you: let's do this together. Let's dig deep and wrestle with the truth while asking our hearts some real questions. Let's refuse to fake it. Granted, discovering together what it means to passionately follow Jesus may get messy and confront some of our belief systems. But let's keep doing it until we breathe our last breath, and let's bring others along on the journey with us.

In the apostle Paul's words, "Whatever happens, keep living your lives based on the reality of the gospel of Christ, *which reveals him to others*" (Phil. 1:27 TPT, emphasis original). As we follow Jesus instead of the ways of popular culture, Christ will be revealed to others.

Let's wade out of the shallows and into the deep. Let's climb mountains and walk through valleys, lurking with mere shadows of death. Let's walk through the narrow gates of life, choosing an extraordinary faith that brings transformation within and all around, "for wide is the gate and broad is the road that leads to destruction, and many enter through it. But small is the gate and narrow the road that leads to life, and only a few find it" (Matt. 7:13–14).

Making It Real

1. Faking it isn't usually intentional, nor is losing the joy of your salvation, but maybe that's where you find yourself as you read these words. If you're in that place, take some time in prayer to simply ask the Father, Son, and Holy Spirit how the joy of your salvation can be restored in your life. Try recalling the moment of your salvation or a time when you came to a deep revelation of Jesus's love for you. What did it feel like? What do you remember? What truth revealed dispelled the lies you believed? Write them down and take a moment to simply give gratitude to God for rescuing you. Pray that your *why* is restored once again.
2. Is there an area of your walk with Jesus in which you believe you are faking it? Take some time to either journal or pray to get to the bottom of why you find yourself there. What is one thing you can do today to stop faking it and follow Jesus with all that you are?
3. What is one way you can remove the distractions of an on-demand world and prioritize your relationship with Jesus on a daily basis? What things do you find hard to immediately leave behind when being called to move forward by Jesus? Is there anything you need to let go of in order to move ahead?

2

Love Out of Context

Greater love has no one than this: to lay down one's life for one's friends.

John 15:13

My bags were packed. I was about to embark on a two-week journey to New Zealand with my friend and personal assistant, Trish. We had gone back and forth about how many bags to bring, one or two. We didn't want to be over the top. I mean, two bags? Are we moving to New Zealand? The funny thing is once we went through the list of things we'd *need* to bring, we actually decided on two bags. Yes, two bags would be kosher.

So when Trish showed up on my doorstep with only one overstuffed bag, I felt shame creep in—baggage shame. I'd packed two massive bags to the hilt; they were literally bursting at the seams. I had to sit on them to zip them shut. When I saw Trish's one bag, I panicked. I didn't have time to unpack and repack my bags because we had to go. She left me hanging, making me look like a baggage fool (as if that's a thing), and I didn't know what to do. So I rolled with it—literally, because my bags had wheels.

When it comes to love, many of us feel like baggage fools. We show up with too much weight for the journey, unable to run our race without restraint. Other people in our lives show up looking like they have it all together, or at least having less baggage. Should we change or roll with it?

What do you feel when I write the words *I love you* or *You are loved* or *God loves you*? Is cynicism rising? Did you just roll your eyes and flash a sarcastic smile? Or do you feel a pang of anxiety, or fear, even, in your stomach? Do you want to vomit or run and hide? Do your hackles go up, and are you ready for a fight? Is heat tingling up your neck and all around your face? Do you feel disbelief and despondency? Are you floating away to a happy place so that you don't have to confront your feelings about the topic of love, or are you panicking, ready to shut the book and not read one sentence more? Do you feel like you're walking out the front door of your life with two extremely heavy bags, full of way too much stuff to take on your daily pilgrimage?

Many of us have misconceptions about love that have left us disillusioned. When we define love through the lens of our pain or experiences with imperfect humans, that definition, whatever it may be, always fails us. Maybe someone showed up in your life promising one thing in the name of love but then did another, or maybe no one ever showed up. For you, the word *love* could have abuse and secrecy attached to it. It could be that you've walked through a series of broken relationships or rejection, and you're simply done believing that true love exists. It's possible that love and manipulation go hand in hand due to past experience so that when someone says, "I love you," you want to retort, "What do you want from me?" assuming their words are filled with ulterior motives. Maybe, in the name of love, things have been taken from you by someone you trusted that you can never get back. It could be that your trust was broken so often from childhood to now that self-protection has become your first defense mechanism never to be hurt again. What we used to protect ourselves as children, because we genuinely had no other choice, often becomes detrimental when we're adults if we keep doing the same thing over and over again.

Love is a loaded word, good or bad, for most of us.

As followers of Jesus, we walk in a crazy dichotomy when it comes to love. On the one hand, we have to become aware of the custom-made set of worldly lenses we each put on when pondering love, be they scratched, smudged, or broken by the enemy's strategies. On the other hand, it's imperative that we become aware of the beautiful reality that we are *literally* formed in our mother's womb to be wired for love, connection, and affection. God, as our Creator, made us to remain in relationship and unending union with Him, and He is the very Being of love. This brings me to a very important point: *We don't get to define love; it defines us. We are made in Love's image.* John defines this truth beautifully in 1 John 4:7–10:

> Dear friends, let us love one another, *for love comes from God*. Everyone who loves has been born of God and knows God. Whoever does not love does not know God, because *God is love*. This is how God showed his love among us: He sent his one and only Son into the world that we might live through him. *This is love*: not that we loved God, but that he loved us and sent his Son as an atoning sacrifice for our sins. (emphasis added)

So let's break it down. Love defined:

Love comes from God.
God is love.
Jesus demonstrated love through sacrifice.

Love is the very person of God, who in His good, kind, pure, merciful, and *loving* nature sacrificed His own Son to save our lives from sin, death, and the pit of hell. That is the definition of love—sacrifice, death that brings life.

Love *Does* Win, but Not on Our Terms

If we're in what I call "love lack," we scratch and pine for the real thing, trying to fulfill an unmet (valid) need with counterfeits and defining our own terms and definitions of love as we self-medicate, trying to fill the God-shaped hole in our hearts. Guess what? Our parents saying they're sorry won't fill that hole in our hearts. Getting married won't fill that hole in our hearts. Getting that boyfriend or girlfriend won't fill that hole in our hearts. Getting our dream job won't fill that hole in our hearts. Getting that well-deserved recognition won't fill that hole in our hearts. Marriage equality won't fill that hole in our hearts. Having a baby won't fill that hole in our hearts. God, who is love, can and does heal, restore, and fill the God-shaped hole in our hearts with who He is—love.

We throw around #lovewins and #loveislove, often to further our own agendas without asking the God of love what He thinks about that. We've all used so-called love to selfishly meet our own needs, desires, and agendas. But what if we got the context and person of love right instead? What would our world look like if we started loving well—sacrificing and laying down our lives and agendas to live for one another instead? What if we tore down the false image of self that we've built around ourselves in the hopes that the world will see us how we'd like to be seen and instead allowed love to define who we are? To do so, we first need to decipher the difference between the world's definition of love and God's definition.

Right before John launches into one of the greatest chapters on love in the Bible in 1 John 4, he sets it up contextually so that we can swallow the pill of divine truth he is about to reveal.

In 1 John 1, he proves that Christ is the living expression of God on earth, the "Life-Giver made visible" (v. 2 TPT). Christ is the light, and there is no trace of darkness in Him. This very light uncovers our sins and sets us free. John says that if we claim to be in Him yet walk in the realm of darkness, we're fooling ourselves and not living in the truth (vv. 5–6).

In 1 John 2, John unwraps the beauty of our Redeemer as the answer to our sins. He reminds us that we can be assured we know God if we keep His commands, perfecting His love within us (2:5 TPT). He goes on to speak about spiritual maturity, warning us not to love the things of this world because true gratification in every way is found in our Father. He references the antichrist arising and that the enemies of Christ have already appeared, indicating that we are in the "closing hour of this age" (v. 18 TPT). He admonishes us about the power of truth and divine sonship.

In 1 John 3:1, John reminds us that we have been called and made God's "very own *beloved* children" (TPT, emphasis original)! He warns against "moral anarchy" (v. 4), saying, "The one who continues sinning hasn't seen him with *discernment* or known him by *intimate experience*" (v. 6 TPT, emphasis original), meaning that our very character and nature will be transformed as we live as children of light connected to the divine. We stop using grace as an excuse to do whatever we'd like on our own terms. Instead, God's unfathomable grace becomes the very thing that spurs us on to the pursuit of purity as we leave our old ways behind. We choose to walk away from the temptation of sin because we *know* Jesus and His great love intimately, and His way *truly* becomes our way.

Then John, "the one whom Jesus loved" (John 20:2 ESV) begins to unpack true love. "The beautiful message you've heard right from the start is that we should walk in self-sacrificing love toward one another" (1 John 3:11 TPT). Yes, he starts with sacrifice because that was how Jesus demonstrated His love for us. As His followers, we are invited to do the same: "This is how we have discovered love's reality: Jesus sacrificed his life for us. Because of this great love, we should be willing to lay down our lives for one another" (v. 16 TPT). As with any invitation, we have a choice to RSVP yes or no. John sets a high bar, and one, if we're honest, we don't often reach for. I'll take the lower rungs, please; I don't want to die to self today. If we see a fellow believer or human being in need and deny them, closing our hearts toward them, John goes so far as to ask, "How is it even possible that God's love lives in him?" (v. 17 TPT).

From this foundation, John breaks down true love, and surprisingly, it comes under the subheading "A Warning Against False Teaching" (TPT), indicating that there are false teachers everywhere making things up about love and leading people astray. Thank goodness John tells us how to recognize the spirit of falsehood and the spirit of truth in regard to this very topic, along with others. In 1 John 4, he says:

> Delightfully loved friends, don't trust every spirit, but *carefully examine what they say to determine if they are of God*, because many false prophets have mingled into the world. Here's the test for those with the genuine Spirit of God: they will confess Jesus as the Christ who has come in the flesh. Everyone who does not acknowledge that Jesus is from God has the spirit of antichrist, which you heard was coming and is already active in the world. (vv. 1–3 TPT, emphasis added)

First John 4:5 says, "*They are from the world and therefore speak from the viewpoint of the world*, and the world listens to them" (emphasis added). Followers of Jesus, why are we surprised when the world acts like the world? Why do we hold them to God's standard when they don't know Him or we haven't laid down our lives and shown them His great love in action? Just a simple thought to refine our potentially judgmental hearts today. Remember, "We are from God, and whoever knows God listens to us; but whoever is not from

God does not listen to us. This is how we recognize the Spirit of truth and the spirit of falsehood" (v. 6). So those who are not yet followers of the Way speak from the viewpoint of the world, even when it comes to the subject of love. When we are following Jesus, the Spirit of truth leads us.

To be clear, we are all *from* God whether we acknowledge it or not. There is a Creator over all of the created, yet not all of creation acknowledges Him—*yet*. Remember, Jesus said, "I am the way and the truth and the life. No one comes to the Father except *through* me" (John 14:6, emphasis added). When we acknowledge Jesus as the way, the truth, and the life, we also come to the Father, acknowledging that we have come from God and that He is Lord over all, even our lives. We then begin living *His* way, with Him as our way, empowered by the Holy Spirit. But the waters become murky and we find ourselves surrounded by confusion when we, as self-proclaimed followers of Jesus Christ, act as though we can keep on living and define love however we want, without laying everything down and asking the God of love what He thinks. We cross over a line and walk into a spirit of falsehood, faking it and deceiving ourselves and others in the process. Friends, following Jesus will cost us everything. It's no longer we who live, but Christ who lives within us (Gal. 2:20). And if that is the case, our ways need to get out of *His* way.

John continues:

> No one has ever seen God; but if we love one another, God lives in us and his love is made complete in us. This is how we know that we live in him and he in us: He has given us of his Spirit. And we have seen and testify that the Father

> has sent his Son to be the Savior of the world. If anyone acknowledges that Jesus is the Son of God, God lives in them and they in God. And so we know and rely on the love God has for us. (1 John 4:12–16)

The context of this *entire* chapter is so important. We quote "love one another" or "all we need is love" (yes, I'm aware this is not a verse but from a Beatles song) without breaking down what that actually means. When we love one another, the very character and nature of God is seen in us—we become love for others. This is evidence that we are created by love and for love, but how do we know if it's God's love or our definition of love? If we are living in Him and He is living in us, then He has given us His Spirit, and His Spirit proves, or testifies, to us that He (in His great love) sent His Son to rescue the entire world from death, destruction, and hell. When we acknowledge that Jesus is the Son of God and turn from our ways of self-preservation and partnership with the enemy, then God—who is love—lives in us and we in God. We are made completely new and begin to come into alignment with the truth as we embrace and walk in our new Christlike nature.

To deny the incarnation of God in His Son Jesus Christ is to deny the author of love access to our lives. When we don't know Jesus as our great rescuer from death and destruction, we'll keep defining love for ourselves by our experience, bias, and pain while keeping the real thing at arm's length. We will continue filling our insatiable desire for love with counterfeit after counterfeit, unsatisfied until we receive the genuine article. We have a God-shaped hole in our hearts that can be filled only by God and His love.

Friends, "*God is love*" (1 John 4:16). Period. There's our definition.

We don't have the luxury of manipulating God, aka Love, into our little box of needs, desires, labels, and classifications. This is when love is taken *out* of context. To put love back into its proper context, we have to realize that God is who He is (Love) and already knows what we need, and He will fulfill, restore, and redeem every single thing through Jesus. To receive from Him instead of the world, we need to turn and acknowledge Him, lay down our lives completely and daily, pick up our cross, and follow Him in resurrection life.

John goes on to say, "Whoever lives in love lives in God, and God in them. This is how love is made complete among us so that we will have confidence on the day of judgment: In this world we are like Jesus" (1 John 4:16–17). I'd love to tell you that there will be no day of judgment, that everyone is already saved and following Jesus; they just don't know it yet. But unfortunately (or fortunately for those who read them), these words are very clear, and so are the prior verses. It is His *kindness*, friends, let me say it again, the *kindness* of God, that leads us to repentance (a turning from our ways and a turning to Him), rescuing us from death and destruction; *this* is why we have *no fear* on the day of judgment. He is good, kind, and all things wonderful!

To recap, the Spirit testifies to us that Jesus is the Son of God. When we receive this as truth, God is in us and we are in God; then we can know and rely on the love that God has for us. This love gives us courage and removes fear from our hearts. This love gives us confidence on the day of judgment because we know we are sons and daughters, loved by our Father in heaven, our great rescuer, who has secured our eternity here on earth and in heaven. "There is no fear in love. But perfect love drives out fear, *because fear has to do with punishment*. The one who fears is not made perfect in love" (1 John 4:18, emphasis added). Do we see that? Fear has to do with punishment! The enemy wants us to believe that *God* is punishing us and that His ways are outdated compared to our modern ideals for love. The truth is the deceiver deceives and attempts to blind us to his deception, keeping us in fear and from seeing the Lover of our souls clearly so that we *think* He isn't good or kind. Isn't it just like the enemy, or the punisher, to twist love so that we never have the real thing? Remember, we don't define love; it defines us.

All the fear we feel of never being loved, held, accepted, acknowledged, seen, or heard—that's straight from the pit of hell. Fear will keep us from the genuine article. Fear will keep us in bondage, creating definitions of love that make us think we are safe even though they're counterfeit. However, when real love invades our world, when we acknowledge this presence that is ready to occupy our hearts—everything changes.

When we receive the real thing, we can then give it away. We've all tried to love someone else without *knowing* true love—it doesn't work. We can only genuinely give love to others when we allow God's love to permeate our very being.

> We love because he first loved us. Whoever claims to love God yet hates a brother or sister is a liar. For whoever does not love their brother and sister, whom they have seen, cannot love God, whom they have not seen. And he has given us this command: Anyone who loves God must also love their brother and sister. (1 John 4:19–21)

If we claim to love God but hate our brother, we're flat-out liars—John's words, not mine. If we live without hatred in our hearts as forgiven and deeply loved children, we won't be settling for a shallow faith at all.

So how does love win? Not because a bill was passed for marriage equality; it's bigger than that—beyond human reason. Love wins because the very Being of love conquered sin, death, destruction, and ultimately Satan and all his demonic principalities so that they will never steal from us again. That's how love wins.

This is how love keeps winning: when every neighbor, roommate, friend, coworker, spouse, mother, father, sister, brother, son, daughter, teacher, and human soul are reconciled to their Creator, to true and genuine love. When we show them who they truly are in Him. When we testify to His great love and rescue and they see love, true love, maybe for the very first time. And when they see it, they see their true selves—made in the very image and likeness of Love—resting in heaven's embrace. When they turn from their ways and turn to seek His face. That's how love keeps winning.

Whatever you may be wrestling with as you ponder these Scripture passages, just remember that condemnation doesn't stem from the heart of God. His love, grace, kindness, and mercy have drawn us near as His children.

> Whenever our hearts make us feel guilty and remind us of our failures, we know that God is much greater and more merciful than our conscience, and he knows everything there is to know about us. My delightfully loved friends, when our hearts don't condemn us, we have a bold freedom to speak face-to-face with God. (1 John 3:20–21 TPT)

Stepping into love casts out fear and condemnation, causing us to live as children of light, face-to-face with God, the way we were created to be.

The Wrong Side of the Comma

Sometimes, even after we receive a measure of truth and revelation about love, we lean back into old habits, performing for love instead of living from it.

Chris Hodges, founding pastor of Church of the Highlands in Birmingham, Alabama, asked this question in a session that my husband was attending: "Are you living on the wrong side of the comma?" It's a reference to John 14:15: "If you love me, you will keep my commandments" (ESV). Are we on the wrong side of the comma, trying to prove our love by keeping his commands, obeying our way into love? Or are we on the other side of the comma, being loved and walking in love?

To put this into context, the verses before and after John 14:15 say:

> You may ask me for anything in my name, and I will do it. (v. 14)

> And I will ask the Father, and he will give you another advocate to help you and be with you forever—the Spirit of truth. The world cannot accept him, because it neither sees him nor knows him. But you know him, for he lives with you and will be in you. I will not leave you as orphans; I will come to you. (vv. 16–18)

In other words, the Father, Son, and Holy Spirit are all on your side, helping you to live *from* love instead of *for* love.

When we live from love, we walk in gratitude and not entitlement. We have a deep sense of security, even when we stumble and fail. We know the difference between consequences and punishment. When we find ourselves being tempted and drawn into sin, we press into love instead of performing and striving. When we live from this place, we allow love, not our culture, emotions, or circumstances, to shape our identity.

Loveless obedience to God's commands produced the older-brother spirit seen in the story of the prodigal son. We tend to focus on the wayward prodigal and how he selfishly took his inheritance, essentially calling his father dead to him in that culture. He squandered it and destroyed his life, and at his darkest, he picked himself up and ran home and was welcomed into his father's arms. But the older brother was cynical and angry that everyone was celebrating his failure of a brother's return home. We'll pick up the story mid-welcome-home party:

> The older brother became angry and refused to go in. So his father went out and pleaded with him. But he answered his father, "Look! *All these years* I've been *slaving* for you and *never disobeyed your orders. Yet you never gave me even a young goat so I could celebrate* with my friends. But when *this son of yours* who has squandered your property with prostitutes comes home, you kill the fattened calf for him!"
>
> "*My son*," the father said, "*you are always with me*, and *everything I have is yours*. But we had to celebrate and be glad, because this brother of yours was dead and is alive again; he was lost and is found." (Luke 15:28–32, emphasis added)

The beauty of the father's great love is stunning. Even when the older brother had built walls of anger, resentment, and jealousy around himself, the father pleaded with him to come and join everyone in celebration. Have you ever been there? Throwing a tantrum *while* the Father is inviting you to come and be with Him and the rest of the family? When we perform for love, and someone else is celebrated, we can't join in because we believe it takes value away from us in some way. The father in the story is in love with *both* of his sons and longs to celebrate life *together*. Our Father is in love with each of His children and longs to be united with us.

The moment the father invited the elder brother in, we saw the son's motives for refusing to do so. He made bold statements: "All these years I've been slaving" and "I've never disobeyed your orders." Let's stop there for a moment. He is far from keeping short accounts here. Self-righteousness will make our sin small and someone else's sin so much bigger. It will cause us to keep a record of wrongs as we ignore the state of our own hearts. The older brother makes sure the father knows how *long* he has been *slaving* for him. Those words really stand out. Do we keep accounts with God, making sure He knows how long and hard we've been working for Him? How often do we do that in relationships in general but particularly in our relationship with God? We think or say things such as, "God, if I do this for you, you'll do this for me, right?" or "God, I've been faithful to you, I've never strayed from your ways, I've shown up every Sunday and served in your house, I've kept all your commands. Now give me what I've been asking for." We don't understand that, as His sons and daughters, we *have* His love and favor—period.

The older son went on to say, "Yet you never gave me even a young goat so I could celebrate with my friends. But when this son of yours . . ." Again, because he is bitter and keeping accounts of how hard he has worked for his father, he can't celebrate his brother's return nor see all that he *already has* as a son of the house. When his father said, "My son, you are always with me, and everything I have is yours," we see the tenderness in his heart and his desire to bring his angry, hurt, and performance-driven son close. This is how our heavenly Father feels about us when we perform for love, compare our lot in life to that of others, and pine after another's calling. He is always standing there, inviting us in to live from love, not for it, and to live from that love in His tender arms.

Our motives and, in turn, our words and actions are conceived within the meditations of our hearts: "Above all else, guard your heart, for everything you do flows from it" (Prov. 4:23). The older son wasn't born angry with his dad, and we can't be sure as to when the seeds of bitterness were planted in his heart. Maybe it was the day his brother left with his inheritance and the older brother thought to himself, *I'm the good son. I've done everything right. Surely my father loves me the most.* And that simple thought, a meditation of the heart, gave birth to bitterness, contempt, and jealousy when the father showed his equally great love for both the wayward and the elder son.

Our heart motives will always surface—we just never know what circumstances, moments, situations, conversations, or seasons will bring them up—so it's crucial that we guard our hearts with intentionality. If we find ourselves operating in an "older-brother spirit," we need only remember the tenderness of the father to draw his rule-keeping son close, inviting him into family and celebration. Wherever you find yourself—wayward, indifferent, offended, bitter, angry, rule keeping, judgmental, or left out—your Father is standing there with deep kindness in His eyes, longing to draw you close.

Love Raises the Standard

Love doesn't mean that sin doesn't matter or that we can misuse grace and do whatever we want: "What shall we say, then? Shall we go on sinning so that grace may increase? By no means! We are those who have died to sin; how can we live in it any longer?" (Rom. 6:1–2).

The profound love of Jesus changes us and raises the standard. When we understand just what we've been saved from, we cannot and *do not* want to go back to the way things were. In John 8, when the woman caught in the act of adultery was sheltered, protected, and rescued by Jesus following her extremely public shame, things changed for her. Jesus didn't say, "There, there. Now go back and keep on living like you were before without consequence." By no means! His great love and rescue called her to rise and change! He called her daughter, seeing her and dignifying her when others were trying to kill her, and then He not only freed her but also said to her, "Go now and leave your life of sin" (v. 11).

When we allow Jesus to rescue us, we choose *daily* to *leave* (walk out on) our lives of sin and partner with our new nature. His love empowers us to do so. Anything that threatens to put a wedge between Jesus and us becomes detestable to us in light of His love and is therefore worthy of being walked out on. We walk away from what we used to know and walk into what is new. The standard is raised, not lowered, with true love.

Love Fulfills the Law

Jesus made the point that the arrival of the gospel of grace did not suddenly abolish the law; in fact, living in love under grace fulfills the requirements of the law.

> Do not think that I have come to abolish the Law or the Prophets; I have not come to abolish them but to fulfill them. For truly I tell you, until heaven and earth disappear, not the smallest letter, not the least stroke of a pen, will by any means disappear from the Law until everything is accomplished. (Matt. 5:17–18)

Grace is not opposed to the law, and here is why. Love is not an alternative to the law—it fulfills it. Loving does everything the law requires and for all the right reasons. Romans 13 says:

> Let no debt remain outstanding, except the continuing debt to love one another, for whoever loves others *has fulfilled* the law. The commandments, "You shall not commit adultery," "You shall not murder," "You shall not steal," "You shall not covet," and whatever other command there may be, are summed up in this one command: "Love your neighbor as yourself." Love does no harm to a neighbor. Therefore *love is the fulfillment of the law*." (vv. 8–10, emphasis added.)

Love is the antidote to everything the law opposes! God so loved the world that He gave His one and only Son to rescue the world from the law—Love went first and fulfilled the law. God fulfilled His promise to every generation. Therefore, when you love others with heaven's motive because you are intimately connected to Love itself, you will not desire to have other gods before Him, commit adultery, murder, steal, or covet. The law is fulfilled by *true* love. All of a sudden, loving God and loving your neighbor as you love yourself makes total sense! When we allow God to love us, we know we are loved; therefore, we can love our neighbors with as much grace and generosity as we give to ourselves. If we don't love our neighbors, we have a love problem; the antidote is to allow ourselves to be loved.

Love Is More than a Feeling

I can't write a chapter on love and not mention that love is more than a feeling. Sometimes loving others and receiving love is just a choice. I know that's not what we want to hear, but it is the truth. Sometimes we *do* feel it, and that's the wonderful icing on the cake of our relationships. But most of the time, it takes our focused engagement to cultivate and grow true, beautiful, and lasting love. It's not surprising that we see love as purely a feeling because Western culture has made it out to be an emotional and, quite frankly, self-centered thing. This way of thinking will only isolate us and keep us from the potential of flourishing, life-giving relationships.

This is what the Bible says love actually is—and it's definitely more than a feeling:

> Love is patient, love is kind. It does not envy, it does not boast, it is not proud. It does not dishonor others, it is not self-seeking, it is not easily angered, it keeps no record of wrongs. Love does not delight in evil but rejoices with the truth. It always protects, always trusts, always hopes, always perseveres. Love never fails. (1 Cor. 13:4–8)

I'm sure Paul and I had this passage read at our wedding, and I'm also almost certain that the moment we arrived home from our honeymoon, I forgot it all. Living this, really living it, takes intentionality, especially on the days we're not "feeling" it. So how do we love like this and grow in love? We choose to practice living it out on a daily basis, whether with an annoying roommate, spouse, coworker, or family member. Being around other imperfect humans is how we grow as we follow Jesus.

Simply put, love requires us to stop thinking about *only* ourselves and to start putting someone else's needs above our own. To engage patience and kindness, to do away with envy of another, to let go of boasting and pride in order to look good to others—these take conscious effort. To choose to honor, we must be intentional. To prevent our relationships from being all about us and what we can get, or "self-seeking" as 1 Corinthians 13:5 puts it, we must choose to grow up and mature. Not to be easily angered and to stop keeping score in arguments require a surrender of our hearts. To rejoice with the truth, we must read the truth and, in turn, believe the best about others. To protect, trust, hope, and persevere with others are daily choices. A life lived changing from the inside out will help us to love others like Jesus loves us.

Don't get me wrong. Love is fueled by passion, but with passion comes sacrifice. We are the living, breathing passion of Christ—"the joy set before him" (Heb. 12:2)—and He sacrificed His life, enduring the cross for our redemption. That is *true* love.

Love *in* Context

The context of love is sacrifice: "Greater love has no one than this: to lay down one's life for one's friends" (John 15:13). In our longing to love and be loved, we forget that love flows from heaven to earth first, not from earth to heaven. There was no greater love than Love incarnate coming down to earth in the form of Jesus Christ to rescue us from destruction and restore all things, including our relationship with Father God.

Regardless of what we've heard, seen, or felt about love—our paradigm *can* change. When it comes to love, we don't have to be that baggage fool, carrying way too much weight around to properly "run our race." However, this change will require something of us. We've got to do the work, partner with the truth, and overcome, ultimately humbling ourselves because pride is venom to love but humility is the antivenom.

Jesus's love is not wasted and the value of His love does not change, whether we receive it or not. He sacrificed for you, whether you acknowledge it or not, whether you pick up your cross and follow Him or not.

Making It Real

1. Read through 1 John and 1 Corinthians 13:4–8 for yourself. What stands out to you? Take some time—a week or two even—to journal, write things that stand out to you on 3 x 5 cards, and take them with you to work or place them somewhere you'll see them every day. Meditate on what true love is and how it can be activated in your life.
2. Are there misconceptions or lies that you've believed about love that God is unearthing? Think about what areas of your life are governed by fear and how the enemy is trying or has tried to use that fear to twist your

definition of love. What does Scripture say in answer to your fears or misconceptions?

3. Are there any areas of your life in which you are living on the wrong side of the comma, like the older brother in the parable of the prodigal son? Where have you allowed bitterness, performance, comparison, or entitlement to create a wall between you and God? Is there anything you need to repent of? Ask forgiveness for? Take some time to go there with God. Allow Jesus's life to reveal to you the way in which to live. Let the Holy Spirit minister to you and tell you just how valuable you are.

3

Identity Crisis

> If you have really experienced the Anointed One, and heard his truth, it will be seen in your life; for we know that the ultimate reality is embodied in Jesus!
>
> Ephesians 4:21 TPT

When I was in kindergarten, I had very short hair, a "boy cut" as I called it. I refused to let my mom do my hair, pick out my clothes, or put me in dresses—unless it was Easter—because you couldn't hang upside down on the monkey bars in a dress! One morning at school, I grabbed the hall pass to go and use the restroom. As I put my hand on the door of the girls' bathroom, a passing student stopped me and said, "You're a boy—you can't go in there."

Adrenaline shot through my body and shame surrounded me. My heart felt tight as fear gripped me. In that moment when she called me a boy, publicly shaming me for going into the girls' bathroom, I instantly questioned my identity. My thoughts ran wild. I mean, my nickname was Andi and I had short hair and preferred unmatched, wrinkly clothes, but I had a vagina. Confusion set in. I shyly said back to her, "No, I'm not. I'm a girl." She responded, "No! You're a boy, and you shouldn't be going in there." I started to cry, turned my back to her, and with my head down in shame pushed open the door and went in anyway.

As I sat there on the toilet, my thoughts wildly pinged off one another. I felt sick to my stomach. At the core of it all, I felt ashamed to be me and questioned the legitimacy of my femininity. I wanted to sit in that stall for the rest of the day, hiding from everyone at the school. In a matter of just a few minutes, I was confused as to who I was. Would people know what she said? I felt like they all knew. Would they question the validity of my being a girl? What was I supposed to do? The other girl's voice was screaming louder in that moment than God's intrinsic voice that had created my inmost being, making me female, powerful, and beautiful.

I went back to the classroom to finish out the day, quietly going inside myself. Though I was naturally outgoing, my voice was momentarily silenced as my thoughts turned destructive, constructing walls to protect my vulnerable, accused heart. I wasn't sure who I was anymore.

I vividly remember a conversation I had with my mom later that day. I was sitting on the toilet at home when she walked in. I said to her, "I'm a boy, Mom." She smiled lovingly at me and said, "Oh, sweetheart, no you're not. You're a beautiful little girl." No shame, just love and truth. I looked down and, void of a penis, I realized she was right. My mom always encouraged me to be me. She relished my tomboy nature and my short, messy hair. She loved my boyish, playful nickname. She cheered me on in all my sports endeavors and my weird fashion choices. She saw the real me and always tried her best to pull out my true identity. She didn't compare me to my brothers or sister but saw me for me and loved me in all my flaws, fire, independence, tenderness, and questioning. Her love consistently led me back to the truth of my identity found in the heartbeat of my Creator—the heartbeat I heard at nineteen, forever drawing me home and solidifying who I truly was.

I think about the fact that I was molested by a man I trusted when I was three and four years old. I remember feeling that men can't be trusted and that I needed to protect myself. Yet in a confusing plot twist, I desired the attention of any man who would give it to me, and I went after it in unhealthy ways. The enemy doesn't wait until we're old enough to process our emotions, thoughts, and feelings properly; he starts targeting our identity at our first breath. I was only five when the student who was just passing by called me a boy. For me, the slow deconstruction of trust in God, man, and humanity started at a young age.

Think for a moment about what people have called you, maybe even from a young age. Has it become a part of your identity, even if you were unaware, because it met some unfulfilled need? Have you swung to the opposite extreme of what someone has called you in an effort to break free of what they said and to unconsciously prove a point? What have people expected of you, be it false or unrealistic expectations? Have their expectations made you feel like a failure? What about those who have told you what you *should* be doing or where you *should* be in life at your age? What has that done to bring destruction? The devil doesn't play—he is unfair, unkind, and unrelenting in his assault. *But God* shows us a way to face our painful experiences or those we've dismissed from our minds to find His heart and, in turn, our true identity in Him. He doesn't want us to fake it, wearing someone else's or the accuser's false identity or expectation of us; He wants to lead us home and show us our intrinsic value—His imprint in us. He holds our identity and purpose.

So now let me ask you, Who does God say that you are? Seriously. Stop, pause, and listen. . . . Do you believe Him? Can you come into agreement with Him? You may have to first dig out some deep-rooted lies to transplant the truth—but doing so is worth the effort. Lies hold you captive. God's truth, not the world's "truth," sets you free to be you.

Identity Is an Inside Job

In our human nature, we're an image-conscious, goal-driven, and self-preserving people and have been since the fall of man, when Satan deceived us to look to ourselves instead of to God for who we are and what we need. I often have conversations with our kids in which I explain that the spiritual world is more real than the ground we place our feet on because this world will fade away, but our spirits, the essence of who we are, will remain alive forever. That said, we *are* made of flesh and blood in the image of God—this was not a mistake on God's part; it was deliberate. But if we're not intentional, we'll forget where we came from and where we're going once we breathe our last breath. We'll also forget whom we belong to and that we were created *for* Him. So are we faking it, constructing our own identity, or are we following Jesus into the arms of our Creator, who holds our true identity in His hands?

Unconsciously, we allow comparison and outward appearances to dictate our identity. The apostle Paul addressed the Corinthian church, saying, "You seem to always be looking at people by their outward appearances" (2 Cor. 10:7 TPT). Sound familiar? This is still a problem today. We judge people by the facade we see without going any deeper. We look at perfectly curated social media feeds and people's ability to influence others as a standard we must attain or have fallen short of. We let the number of followers or lack of followers we have determine our value. We are drawn like moths to a flame to "reality" television shows that couldn't be further from reality. We compare ourselves among ourselves and have created a culture in which success (according to man's scorecard, not heaven's) and fame, add validity to human lives. Being known by the multitudes strokes our egos in an attempt to fill an unmet need that only God can fill. Meanwhile, we're lost at sea and don't know who we really are because we now measure ourselves against the outward appearances and successes of our peers. Comparing one of God's creations to another is unwise. We don't have the luxury of rating the Creator's work, yet we set ourselves up to do just that, as Paul reminds us: "We do not dare to classify or compare ourselves with some who commend themselves. When they measure themselves by themselves and compare themselves with themselves, they are not wise" (v. 12).

Author and speaker Rebekah Lyons used her social media account to quote an idea that came up in a discussion at a Q Idea event: "1 in 4 millennials believe they'll be famous by the time they're 25."[1] If you're not a millennial, you may have just chuckled at their expense, and if you are a millennial, you're probably sick of hearing about what millennials are doing wrong. The truth is millennials are getting a bad rap. This is not just a millennial problem. I believe this way of thinking has seeped into the whole of society, including the church. Whether we admit it or not, we believe that being known by others gives us value. As I said earlier, social media is rewiring our brains to look out instead of in. It's causing us to focus on externals instead of doing a deep dive within ourselves and asking God all our questions about our inherent value. Following Jesus means surrendering our *whole* lives to Him, accepting our human limits, and allowing God to divinely direct our paths. Remember, resurrection means that we first must die to ourselves before what is actually in our God-breathed nature can be resurrected. If we don't follow Jesus into His death, we can't be resurrected into His life. Truly following Him and finding ourselves may cost more than we think, but I'll say it a thousand times—it's worth it. Remember the apostle Paul's words:

> And he has taught you to let go of the lifestyle of the ancient man, the old self-life, which was corrupted by sinful and deceitful desires that spring from delusions. *Now it's time to be made new by every revelation that's been given to you.* And to be transformed as you embrace the glorious Christ-within as your new life and live in union with him! For *God has re-created you* all over again in his perfect righteousness,

and you now belong to him in the realm of true holiness. (Eph. 4:22–24 TPT, emphasis added)

This is mind blowing. We are re-created "*all over again* [*born again*] in his perfect righteousness," and we "belong to him in the realm of *true* holiness." Take that in for a moment. Whether we are seen, accepted, or validated by others does not have the power to dictate our value and identity unless we let it. Christ has met every need we could possibly have! We all want to be seen, heard, and loved, and if we'd wake up, we'd discover that we already are! The problem here is that the search for our identity quickly turns into individualistic narcissism that slowly destroys us and causes church leaders to build self-help churches or churches that validate their identity rather than growing radical, saint-equipping gatherings that go out and effect change in their spheres of influence.

Identity Is the Key to Our Destiny

"Identity is the key to our destiny." These wise words were spoken by Avi Tekle, a Jewish believer who has become a friend to Paul and me, and I couldn't agree more. Ephesians 2:10 says, "We have become his poetry, a re-created people that will fulfill the destiny he has given each of us, for we are joined to Jesus, the Anointed One" (TPT). When we are born again, re-created, if you will, our true identity and destiny are born into our consciousness and become clearer each day because our lives are forever joined to Jesus. We become God-conscious instead of self-conscious.

When we don't know or understand how loved we are, we associate our identity with the stereotypes, humanistic morals, labels, and standards of this world or with people who tell us who we are. According to Peter Scazzero, "The vast majority of us go to our graves without knowing who we are. We unconsciously live someone else's life, or at least someone else's expectations for us. This does violence to ourselves, our relationship with God, and ultimately to others."[2]

When we don't know our true identity, we vie for our place in life rather than rest in the understanding that we are created by a God of love for His love. Understanding that our identity is formed in the very image of God causes us to walk in purpose and destiny without comparison, striving, shame, or envy. The devil doesn't come after our gifts, talents, or possessions; he comes after our hearts. His goal is to get our focus on external things and take our eyes off what truly matters, shifting our attention elsewhere so he can slowly dismantle the strength of our identity in Christ. The enemy's target *is* our identity; if he can deconstruct, confuse, and destroy it, we will lack direction and the understanding of our inherent purpose on earth.

We can find ourselves suffering from an identity crisis in certain seasons of life or when major events take place, such as moving to another city or country, getting married or divorced, having a baby or losing a baby, losing a loved one, trauma, betrayal, loss of a job, position, or title; the list goes on. In certain seasons, I've found myself grasping at who I am instead of living *from* the love of God. But the security of our identity in Christ is an anchor in the unavoidable storms and changes throughout our lifetimes. If we fail to deal with or face our circumstances *with* God, we'll disconnect and grasp for a false reality, meeting our internal needs with external things. We'll equate who we are with who and what we are associated to rather than with our connection to the One who knows us from the inside out.

Think for a moment about the tactics the devil has used against you in the past to deconstruct your identity. He's sly, like a robber coming into a home to steal while the victim is unaware, sleeping, or away. He's not blatant about it; yet when he's been in our figurative home, we're usually aware something is different or out of order. But remember, past "robberies" do not have the power to define us or write our legacies unless we let them or allow others to dictate who we are. In most instances, wrestling is involved in discovering and uncovering our true identity, which has possibly been buried under lies, circumstances, and pain, yet it's a wrestling match we should engage in.

From Jacob to Israel

The struggle to become our authentic selves is an age-old story and one we see through Jacob's life in Genesis 25–33. Jacob was born for great purpose but was completely unaware of his worth. He eventually became Israel, producing the twelve tribes, and through the line of Judah came the Messiah, but it took a wrestling match—literally—for Jacob to walk in his identity.

I often find that most of us want to know our purpose before we fundamentally understand who we are. Purpose comes out of identity, not the other way around. We observe Jacob's story with 20/20 hindsight, whereas our personal journeys are being lived out. Throughout his life, Jacob grasped to find his identity at the hand of others. He even put on his brother's identity, like a hairy Halloween costume, to get what he thought he wanted; he betrayed his father in his last days of life and took what *wasn't* his by force and deception. Only through a face-to-face wrestle with God did he discover who he really was and, in turn, his God-given purpose. No one but the Creator could give him that, and it's the same for us. We cannot separate our identity from our destiny.

In my conversations with Avi Tekle, he said there is no word for "presence" in the Hebrew Bible. The word we refer to as "presence" means "face." So when we read, "The LORD make his face shine on you" in Numbers 6:25, it literally means His face, which we could also translate as presence. When Moses said, "If your Presence does not go with us" (Exod. 33:15), he meant, "If your face won't go with us, we're not going!" This shines an interesting light on Jacob's story.

In Genesis 32:22–32, we see that the place where Jacob wrestled with God was called Peniel, meaning "face of God." For the first time in Jacob's life, he didn't look to others, grasping at what he could get, but met God face-to-face, receiving from Him and living to tell the story! God touched the socket of Jacob's hip, causing him to limp for the rest of his life. This was a constant reminder of the wrestling he had engaged in to find his true self. When Jacob refused to let God go, he shouted, "I will not let you go unless you bless me" (v. 26). It's interesting that even in his wrestling with God, the broken part of his character was longing for genuine blessing from heaven. The blessing he thought he wanted and stole from his brother lacked true satisfaction. He found that going about things his way did not satisfy.

Then God asked him his name, to which he replied, "Jacob." And God said, "Your name will no longer be

Jacob, but Israel, because you have struggled with God and with humans and have overcome" (v. 28). I don't always love embracing a season that involves struggling with God, but afterward I walk differently. My "limp" reminds me of who God says I am. Some of us need a spiritual name change, so embrace the wrestle and never walk the same again.

We must choose to agree with what the Spirit of God reveals to us in our wrestling to receive our true identity. As the apostle Paul reminds us in Ephesians 4:21, "If you have really experienced the Anointed One, and heard his truth, it will be seen in your life; for we know that the ultimate reality is embodied in Jesus!" (TPT). We spend our whole lives wrestling with our flesh and grasping at material possessions and affirmation from others. We forget that only the eternal matters and that Jesus is the source of the very life we long to live. This life here on earth is practice for the real thing, when we will forever be face-to-face with God. We *do* have a choice as to how we live it.

Everything Is New

I distinctly remember a time when my son Sammy, still in diapers, toddled down the stairs, followed by a great stench. I said, "Hey, Sammy, you're poopy; let me change you." To which he casually replied, "No, Mom, I want to stay in my poop," as he continued to waddle down the rest of the steps to his bedroom. At the time, I laughed to myself, thinking how we can live like that. We have the option to make changes and live in the truth that we're washed and clean, but we choose to stay in our "stuff," whatever that may be. Jesus is willing to clean us up and make us new; after all, He rescued us from the wages of our sin, which is death. When we're born again, we are immediately delivered anew; the reset button is hit. Then we get to walk out our salvation on a daily basis, choosing to partner with our new nature.

Sometimes those of us who proclaim to be followers of Jesus act as though we have received only part of Him; we settle for bread crumbs instead of feasting at the table that has been prepared for us. I know this because it has been me. We stay locked up in our prisons, pain, and garbage when we have freedom and a breathtaking inheritance in Jesus. We figuratively choose to stay in our poop when we've already been washed clean and made new. Paul says:

> Before the coming of this faith, we were held in custody under the law, locked up until the faith that was to come would be revealed. So the law was our guardian until Christ came that we might be justified by faith. Now that this faith has come, we are no longer under a guardian. So in Christ Jesus you are all children of God through faith, for all of you who were baptized into Christ have clothed yourselves with Christ. There is neither Jew nor Gentile, neither slave nor free, nor is there male and female, for you are all one in Christ Jesus. If you belong to Christ, then you are Abraham's seed, and heirs according to the promise. (Gal. 3:23–29)

We are heirs to the promise given to Abraham. In essence, God signed a contract with Abraham to which we are the beneficiaries. We find the details of this covenant or contract in Genesis 17, where we see that it was sealed by blood (circumcision) and then ultimately fulfilled by Jesus's sacrifice and blood once for all. God told Abraham that he would be the father of many nations. That nations and kings would come from him. That the covenant He was making with Abraham would be everlasting between Him and his descendants after him for generations to come. That God would be the one and only God to all his descendants. Four hundred thirty years after this covenant was made between Abraham and God, angels were sent to Moses to give him the law, so that he became our mediator until the final mediator, Jesus Christ, came to fulfill the law and reconcile *all* things.

The law of Moses did not supersede the promise given to Abraham, so why was it given? "It was meant to be an intermediary agreement added after God gave the promise of the coming One! It was given to show men how guilty they are, and it remained in force until the Seed was born to fulfill the promises given to Abraham" (Gal. 3:19 TPT). The law was simply proof that we needed a Savior to fulfill the promise given to Abraham. When we live a law-based existence, we become a religious people, annulling the life-giving relationship we already have with Jesus. We can't do this life without Jesus! He connects us back to Father God, our life giver, causing us to cry out, "Abba! Father!"

When we live by the flesh *first*, we die by the flesh, but when we realize we are heirs to a spiritual promise that has lasted for generations, we begin to live differently, as God-conscious children of the living God:

> For those who are led by the Spirit of God are the children of God. The Spirit you received does not make you slaves, so that you live in fear again; rather, the Spirit you received brought about your adoption to sonship. And by him we cry, "Abba, Father." The Spirit himself testifies with our spirit that we are God's children. Now if we are children, then we

> are heirs—heirs of God and co-heirs with Christ, if indeed we share in his sufferings in order that we may also share in his glory. (Rom. 8:14–17)

Do you see that? We're adopted into the very line of Abraham. Now, the God of Abraham, Isaac, and Jacob is *our* God too because of the promise He made. We are no longer orphans or slaves to sin! We are no longer fakes but followers—beloved sons and daughters—of Jesus Christ.

In the Gospels, we see that Jesus came first to His own people, Israel, because they had been groomed and prepared for Him. However, their rejection of the Messiah opened the door to the gentiles—every nation, tribe, tongue, and background—and connects us back to our Creator, the giver of our identity. He is our inheritance, our very great reward. Everything is now new, including the very fabric of our missing identity, as Paul writes:

> Yet look at you now! Everything is new! Although you were once distant and far away from God, now you have been brought delightfully close to him through the sacred blood of Jesus—you have actually been united to Christ!
>
> Our reconciling "Peace" is Jesus! He has made Jew and non-Jew one in Christ. By dying as our sacrifice, he has broken down every wall of prejudice that separated us and has now made us equal through our union with Christ. Ethnic hatred has been dissolved by the crucifixion of his precious body on the cross. The legal code that stood condemning every one of us has now been repealed by his command. His triune essence has made peace between us by starting over—forming one new race of humanity, Jews and non-Jews fused together! (Eph. 2:13–15 TPT)

If Jesus is our reconciling peace, what has He reconciled us to? Our true, created identity and purpose from the foundations of the earth! We are born into people groups, tribes, tongues, and nations. We don't choose the color of our skin or the family we came from or the nation we are born into. But this one thing is true: each and every one of us reflects God's creative genius. When we accept the sacrificial love of God through the death, blood, and resurrection of His Son, Jesus, we individually become new and we corporately become one with the family of God, the body of Christ all around the earth. Our identity is sealed and secure in Christ, and then we go on a journey, hand in hand with our Redeemer, rediscovering who we truly are in Him. What a breathtaking inheritance we have—let's choose to live fully alive in this truth!

We are reconciled to God and then to one another.

> Therefore, if anyone is in Christ, the new creation has come: The old has gone, the new is here! All this is from God, who reconciled us to himself through Christ and gave us the ministry of reconciliation: that God was reconciling the world to himself in Christ, not counting people's sins against them. And he has committed to us the message of reconciliation. We are therefore Christ's ambassadors, as though God were making his appeal through us. We implore you on Christ's behalf: Be reconciled to God. God made him who had no sin to be sin for us, so that in him we might become the righteousness of God. (2 Cor. 5:17–21)

We are reconciled reconcilers.

This is the *good* news—news that stops us from settling for a shallow faith and causes us to dig deeper. As we walk in our unique, God-given identity, we can't help but be changed and change the world.

Made for More

I want more, but not more things of this world. There is a deep longing in me that is never fulfilled, never satisfied, always on the search for great treasure and mystery. C. S. Lewis said, "If we find ourselves with a desire that nothing in this world can satisfy, the most probable explanation is that we were made for another world."[3] I frequently live with a holy dissatisfaction, longing for something that cannot be quenched fully until I stand face-to-face with Jesus.

Eternity has been placed in our hearts (Eccles. 3:11), but we can't fully fathom the depths and mystery of the eternal. We can't fully grasp what God is doing from beginning to end. Our lives on this earth are practice for the real thing—eternity. It's why there is a homing beacon in every heart. Think about a friend who isn't walking with God at the moment. They're searching, desperate to fill an eternal, Jesus-shaped hole in their heart, and they'll do it at any cost. Think about your own life and how you self-medicate with your vice of choice even when you *do* have Jesus.

Each of us is broken in some way. Each of us has had something taken from us that has brought confusion and wounding. Life here on earth isn't always easy, that's for sure. But have you ever noticed that you long for something real? You long to be truly loved, seen, heard? It's because of that Jesus-shaped hole in your heart. It can only be filled by the very Being of love—your Creator, the One your spirit will commune with after this life ends. He adores you and wants to show you and tell you who you really are. You are created in His likeness to walk with Him.

When we start to follow Jesus and refuse to settle for a shallow faith, we realize that we are no longer of this world. It's a little like taking the red pill in the classic movie *The Matrix* that allowed Neo to walk in knowledge and freedom but also awakened him to the brutal truth of the state of the world around him; following Jesus causes us to face the reality of what we see before us while we walk in tension with the revelation that we're made for something much greater. The disparity can be eye opening, but we become resolute; no turning back. We begin to realize that a lot of us have figuratively taken the blue pill instead, choosing to forget and remain numb to reality, letting external circumstances control our identities and destinies. We find ourselves wading in shallow faith up to our ankles, when there's a deep ocean before us, calling us out to more.

Lose Yourself to Find Yourself

The enemy wants to confuse whose we are and what we're made for. We are created by the very Being of love to be radical recipients of that love. We are made for more than what we can see with our eyes and grasp with our bare hands. To discover the eternal in our lives means laying them down daily, picking up our cross, and breaking ties with a false self and false securities.

> Then Jesus said to his disciples, "Whoever wants to be my disciple must *deny themselves* and take up their cross and follow me. For whoever wants to save their life will lose it, but whoever loses their life for me will find it. What good

> will it be for someone to gain the whole world, yet forfeit their soul? Or what can anyone give in exchange for their soul?" (Matt. 16:24–26, emphasis added)

In his book *The Screwtape Letters*, C. S. Lewis said, "When [God] talks of their losing their selves, He means only abandoning the clamor of self-will; once they have done that, He really gives them back all their personality, and boasts (I am afraid, sincerely) that when they are wholly His they will be more themselves than ever."[4] The enemy wants to make a mockery of us, telling us *not* to let go of the identity we've created in our own strength and then prized. But when we let go of the "clamor of self-will" that Lewis speaks of, we find out who we truly are.

If we're not consistently becoming more like Jesus, we've got to ask ourselves, *Why?* We've got to get to a place of desperation and willingness to lay down who we thought we were supposed to be and ask Him who we really are. Who we are and *not* what we do will live on forever because we are eternal beings created for relationship *with* our Creator. It's time to come into alignment with our new and true identities as we follow Christ: "Now it's time to be made new by every revelation that's been given to you. And to be transformed as you embrace the glorious Christ-within as your new life and live in union with him!" (Eph. 4:23–24 TPT).

Making It Real

1. Have you come face-to-face with the reality of what you've allowed to dictate your identity rather than

allowing your Creator to do so? If not, take a moment to listen to who God says you are. Do you believe Him? Can you agree with Him? Weed out the lies that hold you captive. God's truth, not the world's "truth," sets you free to be you. Write down what you hear and read in the Word of God, and then read it again whenever you need to.

2. When you are in an identity crisis as a result of transition, pain, or something else, do you wrestle with God to solidify the identity He has given you, or do you just settle into what you feel? What do you need to do to come into alignment with your nature, which is wrapped in Christ?
3. Ask the Holy Spirit to reveal to you any lies you've believed about yourself. Write them down. Now ask the Holy Spirit to reveal the truth that replaces those lies. Hold on to and partner with the truth of your identity when the devil's lies bombard you. Consider writing some of the Scripture passages in this chapter on 3 x 5 cards or printing them out in a creative way and placing them on your mirror so that every time you look at yourself, you hear the truth speaking back to you.

4

Crowd Pleasers or Mountain Climbers?

> Now when Jesus saw the crowds, he went up on a mountainside and sat down. His disciples came to him, and he began to teach them.
>
> Matthew 5:1–2

One evening while I was on a getaway in Greece with a group of close friends, we went around the table telling stories of significant moments we'd each had with God. One friend spoke of how twenty years previously almost to the day he decided to ascend Mount Olympus with one carrot, one apple, one croissant, and a bottle of water filled only halfway. He'd assumed there'd be a store of some kind at the base camp at which he could buy provisions, but he was mistaken. So with what he had in hand, he began his ascent up the mountain.

The excursion took him two days, with many twists, turns, and frustrations, but he made it. We laughed as he shared his story, astonished by his determination to climb the highest mountain in Greece with hardly any food or water. At one point he climbed the wrong summit because, in his words, "pride overtook him" as he passed several people in the wrong direction! He finally turned around, took the right path, and made his way to the top, in awe of the stunning view.

As he recounted his story, it hit me that the ascents we sometimes embark on as we follow Jesus can leave us feeling unprepared and overwhelmed while simultaneously requiring us to lay down our pride, recalibrate our direction, and choose to keep moving forward.

We've all heard the saying "It's lonely at the top." Whether we're business owners, church leaders, CEOs, entrepreneurs, stay-at-home mothers or fathers, single parents, or something else, we all face innumerable problems and decisions that must be made. But we don't always have a lot of people with whom we can candidly discuss our doubts, questions, and fears. We like the idea of standing on the summit of a mountain, "at the top," in awe of the breathtaking view, but to get there means putting one foot in front of the other even when we're tired, hungry, thirsty, and ready to give up. It means choosing to keep going when others around us give in to cultural norms and counterfeit faith instead. The crowd, for the most part, stays at a figurative base camp in their following of Jesus, and the few will choose to climb to the summit on the narrow road that leads to life. Following Jesus can be lonely at times as we step away from a crowd mentality and take the road less traveled on which not everyone is willing to go.

Our relationship with Jesus searches our belief systems and heart motives in order to bring about inward and outward transformation. Take the Sermon on the Mount, for instance, in Matthew 5–7. Jesus does *not* hold back when teaching His disciples here. In each layer of revelation, He raises the bar. He starts with the Beatitudes and moves into being salt and light, a city on a hill, and the light of the world that cannot be hidden. He speaks of how He has come to fulfill the law, raising the standard for us as His followers. When He speaks of murder, He makes it clear that unholy anger with our brothers and sisters brings damage to our hearts and lives as much as taking a life does; when He speaks of adultery, He says that merely lusting after another is tantamount to the same thing. He goes on to counter our thinking about divorce, making oaths, and justice—no longer is it an eye for an eye but we're now to turn the other cheek. And we're commanded to love not only our neighbor—that's easy—but also our enemy.

What about giving to the needy and not telling the whole world about it (yes, let's put our phones down) so that we're not associated with hypocrites? He walks through the depths of prayer and teaches us *how* to pray, then how to fast, again, unlike the hypocrites. He tells us how to give and that where our treasure is, there our hearts will be also. He tells us not to worry because even the birds of the air are taken care of; we are to seek first the kingdom of God and everything else will be taken care of. He reminds us that the way we judge others is the way we'll be judged. At the same time, He lets us know that God is a good Father who, when we ask, seek, and knock, won't give us a stone in place of the bread we cry out for. He points to the narrow way that many are not accustomed to. We're also to watch out for false prophets and false disciples by testing their fruit. Lastly, He speaks of the difference between wise and foolish builders: "Therefore everyone who hears these words of mine and puts them into practice is like a wise man who built his house on the rock" (Matt. 7:24). If we are following Him and not faking it, doing what He has shown us to do, we are wise builders, able to withstand rising waters and tumultuous storms.

It's impossible to halfheartedly follow Jesus—it's an all-in life; the Sermon on the Mount reveals this truth to us. We cannot claim to be Christians or followers of Jesus and go on living a nominal existence, merely attending church on Sunday (when it fits in our schedule that week) with our Monday through Saturday looking exactly the same as the week before and the week before that, while taking for granted the bounty of knowledge and revelation we have access to in the Word and in the unbroken connection to the Holy Spirit. Going to church doesn't make us Christians just as going to the hardware store doesn't make us carpenters. What makes us Jesus's followers is what we do with what we've been given.

I've found that Jesus comforts the disturbed and disturbs the comfortable. He challenges the prideful and arrogant while loving and lifting up the humble. He breaks down systemic injustice and rebuilds the kingdom of heaven in its place.

The Significance of Mountains

Mountaintops are significant spaces and disputed places of power in Scripture. In Old Testament times, it was believed that mountains were closer to God, who "dwells on high" (Isa. 33:5), but now He dwells in our hearts. Even in nonbiblical culture, "high places" were set up for idol worship because they were considered closer to the gods. King Solomon, who built the temple of God in Jerusalem, later established pagan high places for his wives, causing him to lose his kingdom (1 Kings 11:11). He wavered between two places of worship until his death. Even around the world today, we'll pay higher premiums for real estate with a better view, which is always on higher ground. Want an ocean view with glimpses of the sunset in Hawaii? You'll pay for it! In New York, if you want an unobstructed view of Central Park or the Hudson River at sunset, get ready to hand over the cash.

In historic biblical accounts, many good things happened on top of mountains. To name a few, it was on the mountains of Ararat (Gen. 8:4) that Noah's ark came to rest, preserving a remnant to begin again. In Exodus 3, God spoke to Moses from the flames of a burning bush at Horeb, the mountain of God. In Exodus 19, Moses met God on Mount Sinai several times, hearing God's promises and statutes for His people and eventually writing down the Ten Commandments and the book of the Law, or the Torah (the first five books of the Old Testament), which set Israel apart from any other nation. Elijah defeated the prophets of Baal on Mount Carmel (1 Kings 18:20–40), calling the people to revere and worship the one true God. The temple mount was the site for the temple in Jerusalem built by Solomon.

In the books of Mark and Luke, Jesus appointed the twelve disciples on top of a mountain, and He delivered the Sermon on the Mount—you guessed it—on a mountain. In Matthew 17, Jesus led Peter, James, and John up a high mountain by themselves where he was transfigured before them. We are told that "his face shone like the sun, and his clothes became as white as the light. Just then there appeared before them Moses and Elijah, talking with Jesus" (17:2–3). It was in this place that Father God proclaimed once more, as He had at Jesus's baptism, "This is my Son, whom I love; with him I am well pleased. Listen to him!" (17:5), confirming Jesus's identity to three of His closest friends and disciples.

A rabbi and Messianic Jewish friend of mine told me that in this moment, Moses, who had carried the statutes of God, and Elijah, who had called people to true worship of God—both forerunners of Jesus—passed the baton on to the Messiah, who would usher in the kingdom of heaven here on earth. In the past, Moses and Elijah had encountered God on mountaintops, and now they were encountering Jesus, the Son of God, on a mountaintop, ushering in the fulfillment of the law and the prophets.

Jesus prayed on the Mount of Olives before surrendering His life for us. He climbed Golgotha, also known as Calvary, with a cross on His back to be crucified for you and me.

Mountains are sacred spaces where revelation and transformation take place.

Are We Mountain Climbers or Crowd Pleasers?

When we approach the Sermon on the Mount, it's important to take note that Jesus was well aware of the huge crowds gathering around Him, and yet He did what seemed countercultural to making an impact: He stepped away from them and started to climb the mountainside. Was it to see who would follow? "When Jesus saw his ministry drawing huge crowds, he climbed a hillside. *Those who were apprenticed to him, the committed, climbed with him.* Arriving at a quiet place, he sat down and taught his climbing companions" (Matt. 5:1–2 Message, emphasis added).

When Jesus said to His first disciples, "Come, follow me," they "at once" and "immediately" left everything to do just that. In Jewish culture, it's normal to be called to follow and be taught by a rabbi, but the first thing Jesus did with His new followers was to heal the sick and proclaim "the good news of the kingdom" in Galilee (Matt. 4:23). Put yourself in their shoes for a moment and just imagine that the first order of business after choosing to follow Jesus was to go and heal the sick and proclaim the good news you'd just received. These guys went straight into the deep end—and we're called there too.

At that time, news about Jesus was spreading everywhere throughout Syria. Large crowds were gathering from Galilee, the Decapolis, Jerusalem, Judea, and the region across the Jordan. Those who were ill, suffering from severe pain, demon-possessed, having seizures, or paralyzed came to Jesus, and He healed them (Matt. 4:24–25). These same crowds of people followed Him to the base of the mountain that He ascended to deliver the famous Sermon on the Mount, one of the clearest pathways we have for truly following Jesus. It was a sermon that the crowds really needed to hear, but only "*his disciples* came to him, and he began to teach *them*" (Matt. 5:1–2). There is delineation here between the crowds and Jesus's disciples. Jesus *left* the crowds to teach the *few* who were willing to climb, come to Him, and hear what He had to say. What could happen in our lives if we were willing to climb and continually be taught by Jesus?

Jesus, being God, saw the beginning from the end and understood the impact His twelve imperfect and underqualified disciples would have on the entire world after He ascended to the right hand of the Father. His ministry to the crowds was important as He demonstrated the power of the kingdom of heaven through healing and deliverance; however, the three years He spent in constant relationship with the Twelve has changed the world to this day. Together the twelve apostles started the church, which we are now a part of, and many of them wrote the letters that we now read and call the New Testament. These two things alone were worth the intentional and consistent impartation Jesus gave to them, releasing them in the end to "Go!" and make disciples of their own—a command that echoes into our hearts and lives to this day.

When Jesus climbed that mountain, two significant things happened. First, He intentionally went to a place that was understood in Jewish culture as a place to meet with God. Did they know He was the Son of God yet? We can't be sure, but the symbolism of them literally meeting face-to-face with God on a mountain wouldn't be fully appreciated until He rose again. Second, I think He walked up that mountain to see just *who* would follow Him; the entire crowd was welcome, but His disciples made the climb.

Addressing Our "Crowd" Nature Within

Crowds are with you one moment and against you the next. If you've ever been to a concert or sports event of any kind, you know the crowd is a curious beast to behold *and* be a part of. Certain songs make us take out our phones, as we sway back and forth singing a favorite song, making absolute fools of ourselves. My kids get amped at a baseball game when the wave starts to come around as we all stand and scream when it's our turn to go crazy. When our team's batter strikes out or quarterback gets sacked, we're disappointed and boo or sigh with great displeasure. When our team is winning, our spirits are up and it's high fives all around, even to strangers. When we're behind, we lose interest, get quiet, and start looking at our phones; if it's the seventh inning, we usually pick up our things and go, avoiding traffic on the way out and giving up hope of any possibility that our team could rally in the eighth and ninth innings. The thing is a crowd can pick up and leave whenever they want; they can jeer or cheer without carrying the weight of the game. The players, on the other hand, bear the burden of wins or losses. There are consequences, good or bad, for the way the game goes.

We've all been a part of "the crowd," and it usually doesn't go well for us or the other parties involved. Jesus understood crowd mentality—one moment they were following Him, singing His praises, and the next wanting to stone Him, throw Him off a cliff, and crucify Him. Mob and crowd mentalities are almost always detrimental. What we do in our everyday lives when the crowd disperses is what counts.

To a player on the field or a mountain climber, not being swept away in a crowd is a daily choice. Players in the game understand the pain of loss and the joy of winning, and it takes extreme effort to stay in the game when the crowd dissipates, loses interest, jeers, and criticizes. Confronting our inner crowd mentality is essential in following Jesus. Let's take a look at a few things that could point to our inner crowd nature.

The Consumer Within

When we operate from a consumer mindset, we tend not to make decisions from a rational or contemplative state. Marketers are banking on the fact that we'll *feel* like we need what they are marketing, so we'll jump online and buy it without a thought of our budget or actual needs. Half the time we forget what we ordered and wonder why we ever bought it when it arrives.

The following passage from *The Next Evangelicalism: Freeing the Church from Western Cultural Captivity* by Soong-Chan Rah really made an impression on me. Rah, a college professor and pastor, addresses consumerism and materialism—the soul of Western, white cultural captivity—as it is applied to "shopping" for a church. He reflects on a Sunday when he drove his family forty-five minutes to their "local" church.

> Even after an American Christian chooses a church, he or she will entertain the prospect of leaving a church because it is not meeting his or her personal and individual needs. How easy is it for an American Christian to approach finding the right church the way we approach buying cereal at the local supermarket? We're looking for all the right ingredients and rejecting churches because they don't have our style of worship, our style of preaching, or our type of people. We're purchasing a product rather than committing to the body of Christ.[1]

Mic drop. Wow.

Now stay with me. We're talking about the *consumer within*, not your divine calling and identity, which cause you to find a home with a certain community of people. We are all created differently, with diverse gifts and talents to meet the needs of the distinct parts of the body of Christ, of which Christ is the head, as active and contributing (key word) hands and feet. Say you grew up in a military family—there is no way that you can stay in the same church community when you're moving from place to place. Similarly, maybe you have a pining to invest in or be a part of missions. Well, then, by all means find a community of people to do that with and contribute to. Again, Rah is hitting a deeper nerve and addressing the consumer within all of us that chooses to take from and critique the body of Christ rather than contribute to it and bring a solution.

Some churches operate on a codependent relationship between the pastor and its congregants. The leaders create a "good experience" for you, and hopefully you stay. If you have a "bad experience," you leave. If I, as a pastor, am teaching you to be a consumer, then I shouldn't be surprised when you act like one. But if I keep pushing you back into the arms of your Father, encouraging you to listen to the Holy Spirit and read the words of your Bible, digging into all that you've been given in Jesus and breaking down the religious constructs within your own heart, then you'll become a self-feeder, transformed in your walk with God and, in turn, a multiplier. Sundays will become a place of community, contribution, equipping, encouragement, and activation, not the place where you spiritually grocery shop for your needs. I understand that it takes reciprocation in this scenario to have a healthy church community, *but* we all individually choose whether we're consumers or contributors.

It's easy to leave a church based on offense, past experience, snap judgments, or "not being fed," as if we don't have the ability to feed ourselves. In the Old Testament, the nation of Israel had to rely on manna from heaven, waiting on God and their leaders to tell them what to do, but Jesus came so we could have direct contact with God. Jesus is the bread of life (John 6:35), and we can "eat from His life" on our own every single day—not to mention that we have the Holy Spirit, who leads us into all truth. The church is a community-equipping center, raising and releasing people to go into all the world, with the goal of kingdom renewal of all things. Yes, church leaders, myself included, need to consciously repent and change their ways when it comes to creating environments in which consumers thrive. At the same time, we can all personally confront the consumer nature that lives within our own hearts.

The Judge Within

Pastoring a church is like voluntarily choosing to be a bull's-eye. I have personally been subject to much judgment, but I am not too prideful to admit that my snap judgments of others' perceived motives and intent have caused damage to relationships and ultimately brought me to my knees in repentance. Sometimes I'm quick to speak and get angry rather than being quick to listen, lacking the grace and understanding needed to recognize that every human being is on a journey. But James 1:19 clearly instructs us, "My dear brothers and sisters, take note of this: Everyone should be quick to listen, slow to speak and slow to become angry."

From time to time I have to ask myself these questions: Am I a contributor or a critic? An owner or a constant borrower? A kingdom culture warrior or a destroyer? When we judge first and understand later, we often operate as critics, borrowers, and destroyers. We begin to bring false witness about others before asking God how He sees them.

Furthermore, Jesus tells us, "Do not judge, or you too will be judged. For in the same way you judge others, you will be judged, and with the measure you use, it will be measured to you" (Matt. 7:1–2). This should be alarming to us—we will be judged as we have judged. I know we'd like to erase these verses, but His love raises the bar; it doesn't lower it.

The Confusion Within

The crowd goes with the trends and fears of this world, but as followers of Jesus, we have a firm foundation and a kingdom that cannot be shaken when the world is shaken all around us (Heb. 12:26–28). When we feel like our faith is in a Ping-Pong match, it's hard to get a hold on things.

Jesus had a plan to stop confusion and immaturity in His body, the church, and to bring unity, clarity, and purpose.

> And he has appointed some with grace to be apostles, and some with grace to be prophets, and some with grace to be evangelists, and some with grace to be pastors, and some with grace to be teachers. And their calling is to nurture and prepare all the holy believers to do their own works of ministry, and as they do this they will enlarge and build up the body of Christ. These grace ministries will function until we all attain oneness in the faith, until we all experience the fullness of what it means to know the Son of God, and

> finally we become one perfect man with the full dimensions of spiritual maturity and fully developed in the abundance of Christ.
>
> *And then our immaturity will end! And we will not be easily shaken by trouble, nor led astray by novel teachings or by the false doctrines of deceivers who teach clever lies.* But instead we will remain strong and always sincere in our love as we express the truth. All our direction and ministries will flow from Christ and lead us deeper into him, the anointed Head of his body, the church. (Eph. 4:11–15 TPT, emphasis added)

In short, apostles, prophets, evangelists, pastors, and teachers are a gift from Jesus to the body of Christ to equip and activate the community of believers to *go out* and *do* the work of the ministry in their day-in, day-out lives. These "grace" ministries operate in diversity of perspective and function to strengthen and bring unity to the body of believers, bringing us to a place of experiencing the fullness of what it means to really know the Son of God, until we all come to maturity, "fully developed in the abundance of Christ." Then we will be attuned to the sound of His voice and not shaken, led astray, or confused because we are in Christ! Maturity takes hold of our lives as Jesus continually teaches us.

I am also reminded of the man who built his house on sand versus the man who built his house on a foundation of rock in Luke 6:46–49. In this passage, Jesus says the way to build our lives on a solid foundation involves coming to Him, hearing His words, and putting into practice what He says. My husband, Paul, once said, "Hearing but not doing is a form of deception" based on James 1:22: "Do not merely listen to the word, and so deceive yourselves. Do what it says." Confusion comes when we hear one thing and do another, or refuse to do what the Word has already instructed our hearts to do.

Sometimes we wonder how we ended up so far from where we wanted to be. This *can be* due to the fact that we let God's Word bounce right off us, in one ear and out the other, or that we're not reading the Word at all and are instead being infiltrated with the opinions of this world. Daily obedience produces a harvest of right living, satisfaction, and joy, even when circumstances in our lives aren't great.

Likely we could each address other areas in our lives that point to a crowd mentality. Take time with God to dig out what could be preventing you from climbing mountains with Him. Keep it personal, write it down, and then do something to make a change. Remember, climbing a mountain is simply putting one foot in front of the other.

Avoiding Hard Things

Maybe we don't climb mountains with Jesus because we don't want to be out there on our own, misjudged or misunderstood by others, or seen as too radical. Remaining nominal in our Christianity seems easier. To be nominal means to be insignificant, and its synonyms are token, minimal, minor, and small, to name a few. Truly following Jesus means nothing less than living a significant life whether among the multitudes or when unseen. Maybe we want to be accepted by others and hate the pain of being confronted, or maybe being a mountain climber or true disciple just feels like too much work. However, Jesus's words from the Sermon on the Mount are a warning to us:

> Not everyone who says to me, "Lord, Lord," will enter the kingdom of heaven, but the one who does the will of my Father who is in heaven. On that day many will say to me, "Lord, Lord, did we not prophesy in your name, and cast out demons in your name, and do many mighty works in your name?" And then will I declare to them, "I never knew you; depart from me, you workers of lawlessness." (Matt. 7:21–23 ESV)

That's a hard word straight from the mouth of Jesus, from one of the most pivotal sermons, on top of a mountain, where His true disciples were willing to go—up to hard spaces and places to hear uncomfortable things that would change them and their ways of living from that day forward.

Look, we all want to find shortcuts, easier ways to get things done, systems that will work in the most efficient way. But following Jesus is a life of committing to mountain climbing, even when others pitch a tent, bail out, or choose another direction. The shortcut of avoiding pain causes greater pain in the long term, just like taking shortcuts and hiding the truth from one another in our relationships erode trust.

There are times when I haven't spoken up or stepped out because I was simply avoiding difficult, messy conversations. But Jesus never avoided confrontations; motivated by love, He engaged them in order to see change and transformation. Sometimes I want to simply hide, isolate, and avoid society, but in the climbing and learning we're changed and transformed.

Fire on the Mountaintop

My brother Parker Green, who pastors a discipleship-based church in Southern California, wrote these words after getting a tattoo of a sequoia on his rib cage:

> Sequoia National Park has always been what the Irish call a "thin place" for me. The solitude and lack of distraction just help me hear God crystal clear. This year he promised me that I would be like a "Sequoia" of righteousness. That innumerable lives would be changed for generations because I follow him. That the way we do church and life would cast thousands and thousands of seeds that would change nations. The funny thing about a Sequoia tree pine cone, it needs fire to open and release its seed, and they are extremely small, considering Sequoias are the largest living organisms on the planet. We take people through the fire of discipleship with Jesus. It's not a manufacturing process; it's far from perfect, but those who are refined bear much fruit. So naturally, I got a huge Sequoia tattoo on my rib cage. It will remind me daily of God's promise and command: "be fruitful and multiply."[2]

We commit violence to ourselves when we don't step away from the crowd, rest, reset, and refresh as we climb the figurative mountains in our lives *with* Jesus to be taught by Him.

Will we remain at base camp with the crowd or climb the mountains in front of us to be taught by the Lord?

Making It Real

1. Take some time to read Matthew 5–7, the Sermon on the Mount, in a translation that really speaks to you. Take it all in and write notes down of what stands out to you. What does this sermon mean for your life today? What can you apply to your life right now?
2. Do you relate to the consumer within, the judge within, or the confusion within in your possible crowd nature?

Maybe you want to add another to the list. How can you proactively turn from a crowd mentality within to a life of loving obedience in following Jesus?

3. Do you find yourself being a part of a church community for what you can get from it instead of what you can also give or contribute to it? Do you need to repent before God? Maybe it's time to rise up and be a solution to any problems you see in your faith community. What action steps can you take to build up the body of Christ? Think about how you can better commit to climbing the mountain of following Jesus in your everyday life along with committing to relationships, a church family, and so on.

5

Misplaced Worship

> From here on, worshiping the Father will not be a matter of the right place but with the right heart. For God is a Spirit, and he longs to have sincere worshipers who worship and adore him in the realm of the Spirit and in truth.
>
> John 4:23–24 TPT

I'll never forget the night that my mom took me to a Tiffany concert. It was a school night, and this ten-year-old was out late listening to the lyrical goodness of such songs as "I Saw Him Standing There" and "I Think We're Alone Now." We were seven rows back from the front on the center aisle, and my favorite memory was when she sang "Could've

Been" while glitter from above came down all around her—oh, how budgets have changed for concerts. My ten-year-old awkward self gasped in wonder, wishing I could be her—a walking glitter bomb with flawless vocal skills to wow a preteen crowd.

I remember being in awe of her as we drove home, verbally processing every moment. With ears ringing, eyes lit up with wonder, and hands gesturing wildly, I told my mom all the things I loved about Tiffany and why I wanted to travel the world as an idol for countless teens. I was going to be a musical artist—I just knew it. Mom tenderly interrupted my dream state and said the most awkward and honest words: "You know, Andi, her poop stinks just like everybody else's."

Why, Mom? Why did you say that? My joyful verbal processing suddenly ended. Now I was picturing her on the toilet, a normal human being, just like the rest of us.

Truth be told, that simple statement has stuck with me all the days of my life. It has kept me from misplacing my worship by putting people in places and on pedestals where they don't belong. People fail; God never lets us down.

Our misplaced worship of self, fame, modern culture, jobs, relationships, emotional highs, addiction, attention, and so on above God and His unending goodness and character is a trap and ultimately a counterfeit in place of the genuine article we're actually longing for. When we understand how good and kind God is and that He never fails us, no matter the season, we stop making worship about us because we cannot help but adore the One who knows us better than we know ourselves. We stop misplacing our worship and return to the One for whom we were created.

Preference over Reverence

People leave churches over songs that are sung or not sung on a Sunday, whether because of genre, style, or artist. Sometimes that's all it takes—your church didn't play your preference on Sunday, as if it's a radio station you can control or you're gone. The hard truth is we've made the church impotent by making it a place we sporadically grace with our presence to get fueled up so we can get through another week when it is *so* much more. We've made the living, breathing body of Christ to be all about what we can get rather than what we can contribute.

Soong-Chan Rah speaks of our culture's narcissism, or what I like to call "misplaced worship," and how it affects the church today:

> The individualized narcissism of our society translates into our church life in not only our self-absorbed worship and longing for sermons that speak to us or bless us personally but even in how we live out our church community life. A therapeutic culture translates into the context of the local church with an individualized and personalized approach to counseling and self-care. Community is lost in the process of a highly individualized approach. Even small group ministry, which is supposed to be the primary expression of community life in the American evangelical church, often yields a narcissistic, individualistic focus. Small groups become a place of support and counsel rather than a place where Scripture challenges the participants toward kingdom living.[1]

Have our gatherings simply become a place in which our personal preferences and needs are met so that we can reach our goals and dreams, while subsequently losing sight of the fact that we are connected to God and to one another? Have we forgotten that the church is to be a place for equipping so that we can go out into our spheres of influence and *do the work* of the ministry—meeting needs and sharing the gospel in our communities? We're consumed with entitlement, defending the right to an opinion in conversation or on our blogs and social channels or to anyone who will listen. We talk about and pull apart the church as if we're somehow separated from it—because we feel entitled to do so.

What about covenant community? A people reconciled to God and one another who are *for* one another. A people who hunger to see His kingdom come and His will be done here on earth as it is in heaven. A people wide awake and willing to do what it takes to see just one more person come home to Jesus. Have we become a people who simply attend a concert, settling in to listen to a speech, flitting here, there, and everywhere to be "fed"? Or are we gathering to ascribe worth, awe, admiration, and honor to almighty God while being equipped, activated, and encouraged by one another to go out and transform our neighborhoods and communities? Yes, Jesus came for us—His life, death, and resurrection were all about His great love for us—but He also came for those who are not yet home and in the arms of the Father.

What Is the Church Anyway?

In Matthew 16:13–20, Jesus discussed with His disciples what the talk of the town was, who people were saying He was. Some said He was John the Baptist raised from the dead, Elijah, Jeremiah, or one of the other prophets. Then Jesus asked a poignant question: "But what about you? . . .

Who do you say I am?" to which Peter blurted out, "You are the Messiah, the Son of the living God" (vv. 15–16). Jesus affirmed Peter, making it clear to him and everyone listening that this revelation was not from man but from Jesus's Father in heaven. And on this very revelation—that He is the Christ, the Son of the living God—He "will build [His] church" (v. 18), and the gates of hell will not prevail against it. The rock on which we build the church is Jesus Christ—not ideals, not buildings, not even our differences in theology but the very life of Jesus Christ. The implication here is *not* that the church will be built on Peter the rock but that it will be built on the revelation of the Christ.

When Jesus used the word *church* here, He wasn't speaking of what we picture in our modern-day culture. He wasn't speaking of cathedrals or state-of-the-art auditoriums, nor was He speaking of the name over the door of the church you attend. He was speaking of His unstoppable following. The word for church here is *ekklesia* in the Greek language, meaning "an assembly of the people convened at the public place of the council for the purpose of deliberating."[2] Jesus used a Greek word and concept to express a kingdom concept and to explain that we, as His body, are a group of people summoned together to aid in governing the affairs of the cities we're placed in as we release the kingdom of heaven wherever we go. That's our purpose as the church! Jesus connected modern culture to an eternal assignment—to bring the kingdom of heaven to earth.

What would our cities, towns, and neighborhoods look like if we gathered for a greater purpose? If you are a follower of Jesus, you are not separated from the church, the *ecclesia* (Latin); the church is you and me and every life that gathers on the bedrock of Jesus Christ. What if we came together with pointed purpose in public places, received council, deliberated on what truly mattered, ascribed glory and honor to Jesus, and then went out from there and made a difference, connecting heaven's heart to humanity in our everyday affairs?

Jesus was boldly saying that He would build His gathering, His assembly of followers, who would be an unstoppable force, and that the gates of hell, the powers of death and destruction, would have no chance of destroying them.

Acts 2 is a timeless model for the body of Christ, the ecclesia.

> They devoted themselves to the apostles' teaching and to fellowship, to the breaking of bread and to prayer. Everyone was filled with awe at the many wonders and signs performed by the apostles. All the believers were together and had everything in common. They sold property and possessions to give to anyone who had need. Every day they continued to meet together in the temple courts. They broke bread in their homes and ate together with glad and sincere hearts, praising God and enjoying the favor of all the people. And the Lord added to their number daily those who were being saved. (vv. 42–47)

Do you see that? They devoted *themselves* to one another. They didn't need an apostle or pastor to coax them through spectacular teaching to stick around and *choose* to devote themselves to apostolic teaching, fellowship with other believers, the breaking of bread, and prayer. They met Jesus and were lit up with His love, and as a result, they chose a *life* of devotion to God and one another. The passage doesn't even mention worship as we know it! They chose to show up *daily* for teaching, food, fellowship, and prayer—no worship set included because they lived a life of worship. They had Jesus in common. They met *each other's* needs (the pastor didn't do it all) so that no one went without and ate together with great thanksgiving. The fruit of all this was seeing people saved and won into the kingdom on a daily basis.

Is our faith about what *we* need, or is it about contributing to a thriving community full of life and love and extending our arms to those who are not yet home? Is it about personal preference or awe-inspired reverence for God?

Sacred Cows

Years ago my husband gave a leadership message about sacred cows. He reflected on the story of Moses going up Mount Sinai and etching out the first draft of the Ten Commandments only to come down and see that his brother, Aaron the priest, and the people of Israel had gotten tired of waiting for him to come back. Because they didn't know what had happened to Moses, they had the brilliant idea of making "gods who will go before us" (Exod. 32:1). Have you ever noticed that impatience often causes us to create man-made idols? We worship our own dreams, plans, and time lines instead of being still and trusting that God is God, even in silent seasons.

The people of Israel gathered their jewelry together and made a "sacred" cow to worship. Aaron said, "These are your gods, Israel, who brought you up out of Egypt" (Exod. 32:4). Think about it. They were literally delivered from slavery through some of the greatest signs, wonders, and miracles, which they saw with their own eyes, and yet they *chose* to worship a man-made golden calf. Sounds ridiculous, but we too do it all the time. We turn to *things* that we elevate above our relationship with or trust in God.

Moses came down from the mountain with two tablets of stone in hand etched with the covenant of the law and was furious with what he saw: a people worshiping a golden calf when they were invited to worship the living God! The first draft of the Ten Commandments hit the ground in a heart-stopping fury, shattering into pieces, giving us a picture of how following the ways of God comes crashing to a halt when we're consumed with idol worship. Moses ground that golden cow into fine dust, dumped it in the water, and made them drink their own idolatry. Intense, but that's how the story goes and how we can choose to spiritually live—drinking in idolatry rather than the goodness and kindness of a loving God.

Are we more in love with our ideas, ideals, preferences, passions, pet projects, traditions, and ways of the past than we are with what God is doing right here and now in front of our eyes? Do we worship culture and self over God, His ways, and the laying down of our lives?

When it comes to idol worship in our own lives, some of us need to go cow tipping. Let's talk about three prevalent idols in today's Western culture. There are many more, and I'd encourage you to write down your own personal idols—idols causing you to misplace your worship—that may need to be knocked down.

Tipping Over Our Misplaced Worship of Self

Do not think I'm not about self-care. I am. I have a day of rest every week, and our family takes long vacations together to refresh and play. I love the spa, and I see a good counselor when the season calls for it. I also have no problem staying in my pajamas all day on my day off, cozied up under a blanket with a good book or watching a movie. However, when the idol of self rises up above everything else, including following Jesus and laying down my life as He did, then I'm starting to miss the point.

Earlier in this chapter I quoted Soong-Chan Rah. It was in his book *The Next Evangelicalism* that I first began to learn and understand more about the idol of individualism. Before we dive in further, let's get a simple definition of individualism. It is "the habit or principle of being independent and self-reliant," a "self-centered feeling or conduct, egoism," and lastly "a social theory favoring freedom of action for individuals over collective or state control."[3]

I wrote an entire book on how to live free, because our wholeness genuinely matters to God—we matter. With that said, we walk in a tension here because our freedom wasn't free and it wasn't purchased *just* for us. The price for our freedom was high; it cost Jesus His life. Then God's explosive power resurrected Him from the grave—the same power that is alive and at work in us (Rom. 8:11)! When we receive Jesus, we receive all of Him and begin following in His ways. He died for every single *one*. He bought freedom for us because we matter as God's children, but the freedom He purchased is also for others. Yet if we prize ourselves over others for too long, we step into narcissistic individualism, partnering with modern-day culture instead of kingdom culture. Rah says:

> This narcissistic individualism of American society finds a direct corollary in the American evangelical church. Our

> church life becomes an expression of an individualism, yielding a self-absorbed narcissism. Instead of the church becoming an expression of a spiritual life lived in the community of believers or a spiritual life expressed in the context of neighborhood community, our church life becomes a fulfillment of our individual desires and needs. Elements of the worship service, including the preaching of the Word and the worship of God, become reduced to a form of therapy that places the individual at the center of the worship service.[4]

The solution to our problem of the worship of self is simple yet challenging: die to self on a daily basis, pick up our cross, and follow Jesus as we walk enveloped in His resurrected life. Yes, we die, but it's so that we can *live* in Jesus's resurrection power when we stop worshiping self above all else.

Jesus also cared for Himself, showing us that solitude and rest were necessary for Him who, as God, humbled Himself to walk in human flesh. Although you'll also notice that His downtime was always for the greater good. He often escaped to be alone with the Father to refresh, reflect, listen, and rest—He even slept in storms, if necessary. He was filled with vision, direction, and the capacity to once again pour out and lay down His life for those He came for.

Tipping Over Our Misplaced Worship of Culture

Are we mirroring our culture or cultivating kingdom culture here on earth as it is in heaven? Social media and our constant access to a digitally connected world are rewiring our minds to look down instead of up. Our culture is consumed with comparison, self-promotion, and overall individualism, and we as the church, Christ's body here on earth, often blindly follow suit.

> The American church, in taking its cues from Western, white culture, has placed at the center of its theology and ecclesiology the primacy of the individual. The cultural captivity of the church has meant that the church is more likely to reflect the individualism of Western philosophy than the value of community found in Scripture. The individualistic philosophy that has shaped Western society, and consequently shaped the American church, reduces Christian faith to personal, private and individual faith.[5]

Individualism and culture are tied together.

Don't get me wrong. Modern means will always emerge with which to get the message of Christ and His love out to others. *But* we need to live with an awareness of when, in our efforts to be relevant, we're crossing a line, reflecting more of modern culture than of biblical culture. I'm not telling you to shut down your social media; I'm pleading with you to live aware of the influence that culture has in your life. I'm asking you to ask yourself if kingdom culture has your heart or if you're captive to popular culture and, in turn, misplacing your worship.

For example, social media in and of itself is like money—it doesn't have power over us unless we let it get hold of our hearts. It's a means to an end, and that end could be connecting heaven's heart to humanity, if we so choose.

The solution in dealing with the idol of culture in our lives is first to be aware that it even exists. Are we dealing with the issues we face in the same way that culture does, or are we seeking out God and godly wisdom on how to do so? Are we jumping on bandwagons without a thought, or are we walking in the truth of the Word before we jump in? Are we taking a ride on the ranting and raving express, or are we poised with a word in season with which to feed the multitudes?

We are empowered to choose. If we live unaware or indifferent, we will blend in with culture rather than see the will of the Father here on earth as it is in heaven.

Tipping Over Our Misplaced Worship of Comparison

While brushing my teeth one morning, staring at myself in the mirror, I became aware of my thoughts. I had begun to compare myself to someone else, which seemed harmless at first until my internal dialogue became like a Ping-Pong ball being smashed back and forth between two Olympians competing for the gold medal. Midthought, the Holy Spirit interrupted me and whispered, "Only Pharisees compare themselves among themselves. You are a child of God."

True confession: as a pastor of a church, it's tempting to post pictures only of our best and biggest Sundays or gatherings. Why don't I post when only the remnant shows up? Why don't I post when there's a disaster and the service falls apart or when an adult throws a world-class tantrum in plain sight? It's straight pride—that's why. I'm simply presenting my "best life," albeit void of any humility, so that you'll like me, literally click "like."

Why does it matter so much? Why do I care what people think regarding what I'm called to build? Why do I hear "audience of one" and giggle, because really I just want a bigger audience? If posting "I live for an audience of one" will get me more followers, then let's do it! And I have a feeling I'm not the only one—can you see me winking? We like the idea that we live our lives for God only—our audience of one—but we so easily partner with the ways of modern culture, misplacing our worship and, in turn, forsaking our first love.

The idol of comparison is pharisaical and rampant in both the world *and* the church. And when I say church here, I mean the ecclesia—the people who gather for the cause of Christ. I know because I have been this Pharisee, trying to run someone else's race only to get my stumbling feet caught up in the spikes of their cleats. I've tumbled to the ground and fallen flat on my face because I veered off course trying to run in the wrong lane.

We shout and scream for affirmation from others, when it would be simple and best if we remained focused on our assignment, being obedient to the Holy Spirit while building our part of the body of Christ. It's a body, not just one big toe or one pointer finger. Why are we all trying to do the same thing? Or look the same? Or measure success by what someone else has done? Or to the other extreme, why are we acting like our way is the only way? The body is diverse, and that's on purpose. It's a place where *everyone* can belong.

In a physical body, some parts are hidden for good reason, while others are seen. The skin is a wonderful organ; without it the body would be a mushy, muscly, exposed mess. The lungs are necessary for breathing but completely unseen; I'm glad I have them. In the body of Christ, what if you're called to be a lung, liver, or pinky toe? Are you filled with a holy contentment or a despairing disappointment with your assignment from heaven?

Obviously, this is figurative, but it's a powerful metaphor that the apostle Paul uses in 1 Corinthians 12:

> Just as a body, though one, has many parts, but all its many parts form one body, so it is with Christ. For we were all baptized by one Spirit so as to form *one body*—whether Jews or Gentiles, slave or free—and we were all given the one Spirit to drink. Even so the body is not made up of one part but of many. Now if the foot should say, "Because I am not a hand, I do not belong to the body," it would not for that reason stop being part of the body. And if the ear should say, "Because I am not an eye, I do not belong to the body," it would not for that reason stop being part of the body. If the whole body were an eye, where would the sense of hearing be? If the whole body were an ear, where would the sense of smell be? But in fact God has placed the parts in the body, every one of them, just as he wanted them to be. If they were all one part, where would the body be? As it is, there are many parts, but one body. (vv. 12–20, emphasis added)

He goes on to say that the eye cannot say to the hand, "I don't need you!" (v. 21). This is actually deeper than just comparison, because we legitimately *need* each other. An arm is useless when it's not attached to the rest of the body. Who's heard of a high-and-mighty arm? Well, we've all been one—cut off from the blood supply and connective tissue of the rest of the body because we think we know best. Each part is indispensable to the rest of the body, *and* "God has put the body together, giving greater honor to the parts that lacked it, so that there should be no division in the body, but that its parts should have equal concern for each other.

If one part suffers, every part suffers with it; if one part is honored, every part rejoices with it" (vv. 24–26).

Say what? You mean if another church, aka gathering of people, in my city has a huge win, then it's my win too? And if another church in my city falls flat on its face, then it's my pain too? Or if people are being martyred in the Middle East for their faith, it's my suffering too? Or if Reinhard Bonnke gathers the multitudes and sees millions won to the heart of the Father through Jesus Christ, it's my win too? Yes! Yes to all of the above. But if we don't destroy the idol of comparison, we will be building churches unto ourselves, for ourselves, and for our glory!

We're all on the same team—part of the same body with Jesus securely in place as the cornerstone of it all. He is the head. He is our why. He is the bedrock upon which we build . . . lest we forget.

Some of you are reading this and thinking, *I'm not a pastor or a leader or building the church*. And here is where I'm going to call you out and up—yes, yes, you are. If you are a part of the ecclesia, you are a part of the body that is on assignment to go out and be the hands and feet to a world in desperate need of encountering the living Jesus through your life. You may be the only shepherd, evangelist, prophet, or Bible teacher that your family or coworker ever meets. If you are wrapped up in comparison in any way—and I mean *any* way—then this all relates to you.

Comparison sets up pedestals that people either fall off of or fall short of. Whenever we compare ourselves among ourselves, we are worshiping the idol of comparison and getting into dangerous spaces that don't exist in heaven. That's why Satan was thrown out—he wanted God's place when it was never his to claim. Jesus taught us to pray, "Your kingdom come, your will be done, on earth as it is in heaven" (Matt. 6:10). If there is no comparison in heaven, then we are to simply pray that the will of heaven will be released here on earth. The holy Trinity is one, unified Godhead and our example of unity. Let's pray that the idol of comparison will fall in our churches and in our lives so that, in turn, we will be a light to the world by how we love one another and are for one another.

The world will know that we are his disciples by how we *love* one another (John 13:35).

The One True God

I could go on with other areas of misplaced worship, but I have a feeling that you know your vice. An idol is anything that takes the place of God in our lives. Are we asking for advice from our idols or from the living God who created us? We've all engaged in idol worship and can repent today and change our ways. This is good news!

The apostle Paul was a brilliant communicator of the gospel to any audience—be it through letters to the churches or moments reflected in the book of Acts through the author. He had a way of addressing culture without tearing down the identity of a people group. He knew how to bring Jesus right into the midst of a people in a way that spoke directly to their hearts.

In Acts 17, Paul was in Athens waiting for Timothy and Silas to come and join him. While he was waiting, he became aware of the culture of the city and "was greatly distressed to see that the city was full of idols" (v. 16). He didn't take this moment to criticize, degrade, and judge the city; he used their idol worship as an entry point for the gospel.

He made the most of conversations in the marketplace with Jews and God-fearing Greeks until a group of Epicurean and Stoic philosophers, who were the representatives of Greek thought at the time, took up a debate with him. He spoke of Jesus and the resurrection, which had not been a part of their philosophical discussions until that moment. At first they mocked him, wondering what on earth he was talking about. Then they were intrigued and brought him to a meeting of the Areopagus, the highest government council and judicial court, and asked him to tell them more of this "new teaching" and these "strange ideas" (vv. 19–20). The Athenians spent a large portion of their lives talking about and listening to the latest ideas and philosophies, and Paul took advantage of that habit to bring them the gospel.

> Paul then stood up in the meeting of the Areopagus and said: "People of Athens! I see that in every way you are very religious. For as I walked around and looked carefully at your objects of worship, I even found an altar with this inscription: TO AN UNKNOWN GOD. So you are ignorant of the very thing you worship—and this is what I am going to proclaim to you." (vv. 22–23)

A leader on our team, Nicole Smithee, taught on this very passage in one of our staff meetings and pointed out that the apostle Paul even went so far as to honor the Athenians by saying, "I see that in every way you are very religious." He won the hearts of these philosophers, then pointed out their ignorance and shared the truth. He had their attention and then brought his point home, pointing out that the unknown

God they worshiped was, in fact, the God who made the world and sent His only Son to rescue them!

> The God who made the world and everything in it is the Lord of heaven and earth and does not live in temples built by human hands. And he is not served by human hands, as if he needed anything. Rather, he himself gives everyone life and breath and everything else. From one man he made all the nations, that they should inhabit the whole earth; and he marked out their appointed times in history and the boundaries of their lands. God did this so that they would seek him and perhaps reach out for him and find him, though he is not far from any one of us. "For in him we live and move and have our being." As some of your own poets have said, "We are his offspring." (vv. 24–28)

Paul told them that if they are God's offspring, He cannot be made of gold, silver, or stone carved out by human hands. But the unknown god mentioned on their altar? That's the God of all creation who sent His Son, Jesus, to reconcile them to Himself. With all that said, it was time to repent and turn from their ways! Some mocked him in that moment, but a number of them followed Jesus and believed, including a member of the Areopagus named Dionysius and a woman named Damaris.

Imagine if Paul had bowed to culture out of fear or ignorance. What if he had made his faith purely individual and personal? He could have used the stress of being in that idolatrous atmosphere as an excuse to run away because it was all too much, and this moment would never have happened! Idol worship didn't worry him; it burdened him to the point of loving others well and sharing the Good News.

Genuine Worship . . . and Why It Matters

Worship has never been about genres, spaces, places, or who has the best sound and voice. We are simply placing worth on the name above all names, including our own name, from the depths of our beating hearts, and it comes out in various beautiful expressions from dynamic cultures all around the world.

In John 4, Jesus encountered a Samaritan woman at a well and had a timely conversation with her that touched on racism, gender, worship, and evangelism. But for this illustration, we will zero in on His statement about worship.

Jesus was talking alone to a woman who not only wasn't his wife but also was a *Samaritan* woman—and Jews didn't associate with Samaritans. In the midst of their conversation, He had a word of knowledge, seeing her brokenness but not walking away. She stated, "I can see that you are a prophet" (v. 19) and seized the moment to ask her captive audience a question that seems to have been weighing on her mind. She asked why her forefathers worshiped at a nearby mountain when the Jews say that Jerusalem is the place to worship.

> "Woman," Jesus replied, "believe me, a time is coming when you will worship the Father neither on this mountain nor in Jerusalem. You Samaritans worship what you do not know; we worship what we do know, for salvation is from the Jews. Yet a time is coming and has now come when the true worshipers will worship the Father in the Spirit and in truth, for they are the kind of worshipers the Father seeks. God is spirit, and his worshipers must worship in the Spirit and in truth." (vv. 21–24)

This is profound. It doesn't matter *where* you worship; it matters *how* you worship and *what* you worship. The Passion Translation says, "From here on, worshiping the Father will not be a matter of the right place but *with the right heart*. For God is a Spirit, and he longs to have *sincere worshipers* who worship and adore him in the realm of the Spirit and in truth" (John 4:23–24, emphasis added).

Whether you're in an underground church without a state-of-the-art sound system in a nation under extreme persecution or in a small community church in the backwoods of nowhereville or in a house church with just your voices or in a massive well-known church whose worship is mind-blowingly beautiful to the ears—*make sure it's about your heart*. Tip over the idols of individualism, culture, and comparison so that you can run to the throne room whenever you desire and wherever you are.

Making It Real

1. What does the word *church* evoke for you? Do you need to look at the ecclesia in a new way? Maybe you need to wrestle with this to see the church with new eyes, to see that it's a body to which you belong and are designed to contribute to, showing the world through love that Christ is the way, truth, and life.
2. Ask yourself, *Do I need to go cow tipping with some idols in my life? Do I have any misplaced worship?* Maybe it's the idol of self, culture, or comparison. Maybe you've begun to worship your marriage, time, things, job, children, and so on, and those things have

taken the place of the one and only God (who gave you all of those things) without you even noticing. How can you put Jesus back into the center of your life?

3. Ask the Holy Spirit to reveal to you any areas of your life in which you have been following the ways and culture of the world instead of kingdom culture. What changes can you make today to see change? Does others' figurative idol worship or misplaced worship burden you, or does it cause you to stand in the place of judgment?

6

Introverted Extroverts

> After [Jesus] had dismissed the crowds, he went up on the mountain by himself to pray. When evening came, he was there alone.
>
> Matthew 14:23 ESV

I'm what I like to call an introverted extrovert. I'm the life of the party, until I'm not. It's like a switch is flipped, and I can't communicate anymore because I'm simply done being around people and just want to be alone. Social labels tell us that we are either one or the other—extroverted or introverted—but to walk in health and wholeness, I think we need a little bit of both in our lives.

If we look at the life of Jesus, we see that He understood the power of purposeful solitude so that He could connect with others and show them the heart of the Father here on earth: He was an introverted extrovert. He was not afraid to be alone in His Father's presence, stealing away from the crowds, but He also lived a life in close proximity with twelve other men, had multiple followers, and often found Himself pressed by or speaking to the crowds. The balance of being alone and in community is imperative to bring health to our lives as followers of Jesus. Dietrich Bonhoeffer said, "Let the person who cannot be alone beware of community. Let the person who is not in community beware of being alone"[1] When either becomes a crutch, a coping or hiding mechanism, we've got to look inward as to why. Solitude, the practice of being absent from others and things, is foundational to our emotional, physical, and spiritual health, and as followers of Jesus, we should pay attention to how He operated.

In our individual journeys of following Jesus, the practice of solitude, reflection, meditation, and prayer is key to living an authentic life; neglecting the emotional and spiritual parts of our being can have damaging effects. Bulldozing through life without properly processing pain because we think we need to move forward or get over it cause us to fake it. Ultimately, when a dark season—major failure, burnout, unexpected transition, serious illness, broken dreams, relational breakdown—comes, we may find ourselves walking away from it all in our hearts and eventually with our entire lives. Instead, we can choose to let the difficult and challenging seasons do a deep work in us.

Purposeful solitude shows us more of who we are, good or bad, and at the same time reveals more of the mystery and depths of who God is—even in the middle of failure, pain, and disappointment. It's important to know the difference between isolation and purposeful solitude. Isolation is self-protection from society, whereas purposeful solitude is preparation for society. Anytime Jesus went off alone, He came back with "food" for His disciples or followers. He had either a shift in direction or the fortitude to continue on with the plan from heaven placed before Him. Are we willing to do the work and take the time to sit alone and self-reflect *with* God to see change and transformation in our own lives and, in turn, the lives of those around us? Sometimes we avoid solitude by staying busy and around people with what I like to call chronic extroversion—or we go to the other extreme, isolating and self-medicating emotionally so as not to face or feel what we need to in order to move forward.

Feeling the Pain Once Again

It was another stormy season, churning with confusion, anxiety, and pain. Our church had gone through some massive changes and transitions over the previous year and a half, and I felt like a failure on every front. Disappointment was never far from the door of my heart. With Paul and I as the captain and executive officer (respectively) of our figurative ship, it felt as though we were navigating an endless storm with no view of the horizon in sight. When people emailed their criticisms, advice, or suggestions—negative or positive—they brought up deep feelings of hopelessness for me personally. My emotions were all over the place, and I wanted to quit at least once a week. After one particular day of feeling sad and being angry with everyone in sight, I came to a realization: though I had counted the cost of planting a church and following Jesus and even kept choosing to pay the price, in my heart I was beginning to resent the cost.

In the middle of this particular season, I was about to embark on a two-week journey to New Zealand to speak at a friend's church with multiple campuses on both the north and south islands. In saying yes to this invitation, I knew I'd be away from my children and husband for the longest time I had ever been. I'd love to tell you that I was sad to go, because that's what a good mother *should* say, but I couldn't wait to get away—not from my husband and kids but from all the stuff that was swirling around us personally in New York. I needed to fall in love again with the city that God had written on our hearts *and* its people—even the critics and knife throwers among them. I needed the space and I needed to heal.

I had a two-and-a-half-day break from speaking, so the church that was hosting me scheduled in a writing retreat in one of the most beautiful places I have ever been in my life: Queenstown, New Zealand. On the first morning of writing, I lay in my cozy bed nestled next to the fireplace, staring at the vibrant fiery red, orange, and purple sunrise over the mountains next to Lake Wakatipu, and I began to quietly weep. A mess of emotions and revelation swirled together in a beautiful symphony that brought rest and clarity to my soul. I was alone but not lonely. The majesty of those mountains reminded me that when I can't "feel" God or hear and know what to do with my problems or pain, He is there *with* me nonetheless—and that truly is enough. I had a knowing and a peace that "this too will pass," coupled with a resolve not to ignore the reality of what I was feeling or facing and how hard this season was. I partnered with perseverance as love and hope began to take hold.

I read Romans 11:33–36 while the sun continued to rise over the mountains *my* Father had created with His very words:

> Oh, the depth of the riches and wisdom and knowledge of God! How unsearchable are His judgments and decisions and how unfathomable and untraceable are His ways! For who has known the mind of the Lord, or who has been His counselor? Or who has first given to Him that it would be paid back to him? For from Him [all things originate] and through Him [all things live and exist] and to Him are all things [directed]. To Him be glory and honor forever! Amen. (AMP)

I saw myself clearly in that moment—the pride *and* the pain—and I saw who God was in the middle of it all—big, majestic even, yet present and oh so personal. He is vast and unsearchable, yet He chooses to reveal Himself to you and to me, cultivating maturity and bringing about healing. He is always there, replacing my pride and pain with His love and faultless point of view.

We all need purposeful solitude to think, feel, reflect, pray, and become mindful of God's love, goodness, words, and character, all of which cause us to see and live with clarity when life feels like it's falling apart. We begin faking it when we allow people or things to fulfill a need that only God can fulfill. Our emotions can be indicators of the state of our hearts. If we ignore our emotions and visceral reactions for too long, we'll become career fakers, avoiding land mines and living from the outside in instead of from the inside out.

We have to find space to heal, connect, listen, contemplate, and rest in our ever-present help in time of need. Jesus didn't fake it, and He needed time alone with the Father. We are invited to do the same.

Following Jesus into Solitude

I have four kids, so purposeful solitude could be deemed impossible and unreasonable in this season of my life. The truth is we're all busy, distracted, and full of excuses as to why there is no time for purposeful solitude, but I'd like to ask you a question born out of love: How's that working out for you?

If we don't have solitude and time for reflection with God, even just five minutes in the morning, bad things can happen to good people. Whenever I feel misunderstood, not heard, unduly criticized, unsafe, overwhelmed by circumstances, or overstimulated by questions from all four of my kids simultaneously, I can quickly go from sweet, grace-filled, loving, and patient Andi to the Hulk.

To fully go from faking it and just getting by to flourishing and following Jesus in this area of our lives, let's take a look at how He had purposeful solitude while on earth. Remember, He is not just *a* way; He is *the* way to live—He gave us the greatest road map for life. I want to break down a few Scripture passages in chronological order and look at the life of Jesus and how He was purposeful in His times of solitude and then see how they apply to our personal lives as His followers.

We'll begin right after Jesus was baptized by His cousin John in the Jordan River when the Spirit of God descended on Him like a dove and a voice from heaven said, "This is my Son, whom I love; with him I am well pleased!" (Matt. 3:17). This public declaration, this backing by heaven, was huge—His identity was made public in that moment, and it led to Jesus being tested. Have you ever been in a place where God restored to you a piece of your identity that had been lost, missing, or pushed to the side? After God affirmed you, whether publicly or privately, were you challenged in some way—not by God but by Satan? Jesus was no different in this aspect.

Purposeful Solitude in the Wilderness

> At once the Spirit sent [Jesus] out into the wilderness, and he was in the wilderness forty days, being tempted by Satan. He was with the wild animals, and angels attended him. (Mark 1:12–13)

While in the desert, Jesus was tempted by Satan in three major areas: the lust of the flesh, the pride of life, and the lust of life.

Satan said, "If you are the Son of God, tell these stones to become bread" (Matt. 4:3). In other words, "Prove it! Are you really the Son of God? [Insert sarcasm.] If you truly are, then do this and show me." The lust of the flesh was to turn stones to bread so that Jesus could eat and be satiated, filling His stomach and giving Himself the pleasures of the flesh. Jesus was hungry, and He was able to turn those stones into bread if He wanted to. He was near the end of His fast, so what's the big deal? But Jesus, in His time of solitude, was fortified in His convictions and passion not to live for His own appetites but to be filled by God alone.

He retorted, quoting Deuteronomy 8:3, "It is written, 'Man shall not live on bread alone, but on every word that comes from the mouth of God'" (Matt. 4:4). Oh, that this would be our response when belligerent arrows come flying at us from Satan to question our identities as children of God! Even in dire weakness and hunger, Jesus found satisfaction and identity in God and His words of life. He had nothing to prove.

Maybe we avoid solitude because we come face-to-face with the mess of our humanity yet forget how deeply loved and fulfilled we are in God. Have you ever heard the tape recorder in your mind say things such as, "If you're a child of God . . ." or "Did God really say . . . ?" We all have, and then we find ourselves going to other remedies to fill a valid need for affirmation rather than reminding ourselves of what God *really* says and thinks about us. If we can still ourselves long enough and perhaps even fast once in a while, we'll be amazed at what we can discover *with* God in purposeful solitude and physical self-denial.

In the second temptation, the devil quoted Psalm 91:11–12 while standing atop the temple in Jerusalem with Jesus, challenging Jesus once again to prove His identity by testing God. "If you are the Son of God, . . . throw yourself down. For it is written: 'He will command his angels concerning you, and they will lift you up in their hands, so that you will not strike your foot against a stone'" (Matt. 4:6). Again, Jesus didn't take the bait, quoting back to Satan Deuteronomy 6:16: "It is also written: 'Do not put the Lord your God to the test'" (Matt. 4:7). This verse relates to Exodus 17:1–7, when the Israelites grumbled to Moses about bringing them out of Egypt and leading them, their children, and their livestock into the desert to die. Their complaining was the fruit of their lack of faith in God to rescue them and give them what He had promised. They wanted Moses to fix the situation by petitioning God to provide water so they wouldn't die. Jesus had no desire to test His Father to see whether He would rescue Him. He already knew the character of God and trusted Him completely. Forty days of fasting and purposeful solitude will do that. You'll see yourself more clearly and that God is with you in all your circumstances.

The pride of life tempts us when we have a need for public proof that we are loved and seen. If Jesus had jumped off the temple to be saved by a throng of angels for God and everyone to see, He could have proven His identity to the watching world, with a reward of outward power and glory. But Jesus didn't have anything to prove. Through His time of fasting and prayer, His identity was secure; He knew who and whose He was. What could this mean for us in our places of purposeful solitude? What if we realized that no one could take from us what God gives to us? What if we knew who we are and whose we are because we took the time to be in the presence of the One who created us to be loved by Him? God *can* fulfill our strong desire for public affirmation, but that affirmation is found in the secret place with Him and is from Him.

The third temptation was the lust of life. In Matthew 4:8, the devil took Jesus to a high mountain to show him all the kingdoms of the world. He said, "All this I will give you . . . if you will bow down and worship me" (v. 9). In essence, surrender your life to me and you can have it all—every kingdom of this world will be yours and you will be like God (which actually was Satan's greatest desire and the ultimate reason for his downfall). Was Satan unaware that every kingdom was already under Jesus's rule? Think about it. Satan wants what we have—to be created in the image of God—but alas, that was not his portion. The moment humanity was created for God's pleasure in the Garden of Eden, Satan came after us with jealousy and vengeance, trying to get us to turn away from our Creator and instead bow down to the one who can only steal, kill, and destroy our lives. He even tried with the Savior of the world, but as expected, he was outmatched. Jesus retorted, "Away from me, Satan! For it is written: 'Worship the Lord God, and serve him only'" (Matt. 4:10).

With some self-reflection, I'm sure we all would discover some idols set up to the "kingdom of ourselves." We worship things, people, ideologies, movements, money, and the need to be seen, loved, and deemed worthy by others. Sometimes we sacrifice others' well-being to make and protect our own way, neglecting family, friends, honesty, and integrity to get what we want and forgetting Jesus's words in Matthew 16: "For what will it profit a man if he gains the whole world and forfeits his soul?" (v. 26 ESV). Jesus made this statement with complete authority because He had been tempted with the whole world but knew He would have lost Himself if He hadn't resisted the temptation. To preface Matthew 16:26, Jesus said, "Whoever wants to be my disciple must deny themselves and take up their cross and follow me. For whoever wants to save their life will lose it, but whoever loses their life for me will find it" (vv. 24–25). Maybe the devil didn't understand that Jesus *didn't* come to take the world by force; He came to love the world and lay down His life as a sacrifice to reconcile every soul and kingdom of this world back to the heart of the Father. The way to gain the world and restore it wasn't surrender to Satan and his ways; it was complete surrender to God. I have to assume that the devil didn't foresee just how far Jesus would go—death on a cross, all for love. Sacrifice for another was so far from Satan's nature that he wouldn't have seen it coming. It seems that this is exactly what happens when we lay our lives down. Doing so is like a secret weapon that the enemy doesn't see coming.

In times of purposeful solitude in the desert seasons of life or in times of fasting and prayer, how can we let the lust of the flesh, the pride of life, and the lust of life search our hearts? Solitude is peaceful but also revealing and calls us deeper into an authentic and power-filled life of following Jesus. We will deal with our need to be seen, heard, and understood and our need to be right. Even our physical needs become less of a focus as we are more and more satisfied in the One who loved us first.

After the temptations in the wilderness, Jesus began to demonstrate unprecedented signs, wonders, and miracles. The kingdom of heaven was being revealed through His life. His purposeful solitude, fasting, prayer, and self-denial brought Him to an emptying of Himself and the tangible release of the power of God. His life lovingly shows us the way to live. Ask yourself, *Am I desperate to rely on every word that pours from the mouth of God?*

Finding Direction in Purposeful Solitude

Raise your hand if you're a morning person. Okay, I didn't see you, but either you're really proud of yourself right now because you're in the cool club or you just rolled your eyes as you read this page—at midnight—because you're *not* a morning person. It seems that Jesus *was* a morning person, and at times found direction in purposeful solitude while it was still early in the morning:

> Very early in the morning, while it was still dark, Jesus got up, left the house and went off to a solitary place, where he prayed. (Mark 1:35)

The evening before this morning mountaintop prayer, people had been bringing the sick and demon-possessed to the doorstep of Simon's mother-in-law. She had just been healed of a fever by Jesus, and the multitudes wanted Him to do the same for them. Jesus didn't turn anyone away, healing those with various diseases and driving out demons. But the very next morning, He didn't take time to sleep in; instead, He got up early and went to a solitary place to pray. The disciples found Jesus and informed Him that "everyone" was looking for Him. He didn't get caught up in the extreme use of the word "everyone," nor did He feel guilty for getting away by Himself after a big night. Instead, He replied with direction for the next leg of their journey together. He let the disciples know that they were going to change direction and go somewhere else, the nearby villages, so He could continue to preach, stating, "That is why I have come" (Mark 1:38).

Are we looking for direction in our lives in all the wrong places? Jesus stole away to hear from the Father and to learn which way to go next, and then He simply went. Are we willing to take the time to hear from heaven for our lives? Why do we want someone to tell us what to do, where to go, or what our calling is when our Creator is very willing to fill that gap?

Purposeful Solitude on the Mountainside

> Jesus went out to a mountain side to pray, and spent the night praying to God. When morning came, he called his disciples to him and chose twelve of them, whom he also designated apostles. (Luke 6:12–13)

There is something about getting away from it all and getting fresh perspective. My time in Queenstown was a mountainside time of prayer, reflection, and writing—the house was literally nestled on a mountainside. Out of a place of prayer, Jesus called His disciples to Him, and not only that but also chose the twelve apostles from them, the twelve who would change the world and birth the church that we are now a part of. Mountainside prayer is powerful.

If you can, one to two times a year, get away on a little retreat, connect with God, and be filled with fresh vision, purpose, reflection, and direction and maybe even a little healing for your heart. It doesn't have to be on a mountainside in Queenstown, New Zealand—although it comes highly recommended. It can be at a hotel in your hometown, a camping trip in the mountains, a bed and breakfast, or the house of an out-of-town friend. With kids and demanding jobs, it can be hard to find these times, but this form of purposeful solitude resets us and gives us clarity in ways that merely pushing through the seasons of life just can't. It can keep us from running away from it all permanently—"mountainside solitude" is preventative care and good for our emotional and spiritual health.

Purposeful Solitude to Be Refreshed

> After [Jesus] had dismissed the crowds, he went up on the mountain by himself to pray. When evening came, he was there alone. (Matt. 14:23 ESV)

This verse makes me laugh a little bit because there are times when this momma sends herself to a time-out. And when evening comes, I'm still in my bedroom alone—with the door locked. Even Jesus needed solitude for the sake of refreshing His soul, and by evening, "*he was still there alone.*" I appreciate that we see this detail, because sometimes I need just a little more introversion time away from the crowds to get perspective and be refreshed.

John 7:10 says, "After his brothers had gone up to the feast, then [Jesus] also went up, not publicly but in private" (ESV). It was about a ninety-mile walk from Galilee to Jerusalem, nearly five days' worth of walking, giving Jesus plenty of solitude to think and pray. His brothers had just been criticizing him for not wanting to walk through Judea to get to Jerusalem for the Festival of Tabernacles because the Jewish leaders were looking for a way to kill him. They mocked Him, saying, "No one who wants to become a public figure acts in secret. Since you are doing these things [miracles such as feeding the five thousand and walking on water], show yourself to the world" (v. 4). He was firm, letting them know His time was "not yet here" (v. 6) and telling them to go to the festival without Him while He stayed in Galilee. After they left, however, He went also, not publicly but alone and in secret.

It appears that Jesus needed this time to Himself because the Jewish leaders were watching for Him, plotting how to catch Him in a trap, and rumors were running rampant, some saying He was a good man and others saying He was a deceiver (vv. 11–12).

Have you ever been in a similar space? Where you just need to be alone to be refreshed and clear your mind in a time of swirling confusion and accusation? Jesus knew what He needed, even though His brothers were pushing Him to do things their way. And sometimes our purposeful solitude sets us up to walk into a storm of accusations and pressure from others with renewed and clear insight. Jesus knew what He needed, and He took the time to do it—five days, to be precise.

Purposeful Solitude for Others

> One day Jesus was praying in a certain place. When he finished, one of his disciples said to him, "Lord, teach us to pray." (Luke 11:1)

I love the purpose for Jesus's time of prayer here. After He'd finished praying, the disciples asked Him to teach them how to pray, and teach them He did. This is where the Lord's Prayer comes from. After His time praying in a "certain place," He had "food" to give His disciples. It's so easy for us to get into spaces of tiredness and weariness with nothing left to give to others. Yet Jesus shows us the way to live because He is the way. As we follow Jesus into purposeful solitude, prayer, and reflection, we are filled with something eternal to give away, allowing us to be fully present and engaged with others.

The Daily Office of Purposeful Solitude

> When [Jesus and his disciples] had sung a hymn, they went out to the Mount of Olives. (Mark 14:26)

The Mount of Olives was Jesus's "usual" place to pray when he was in Jerusalem (Luke 22:39). Do you have a usual place to pray and steal away? A safe space or quiet place you can go to? Or maybe it's a certain time of day. I wonder how often Jesus went there? I wonder how it felt for Him to go to a familiar space? In our overstimulated culture, we've lost the art of the spiritual disciplines or what I've heard called the Daily Office.

I love how the forty-day devotional *Emotionally Healthy Spirituality Day by Day* breaks down what the term *Daily Office* means and how there is power in prioritizing and setting aside a usual space and time to connect with God daily.

> So why is it called the "Daily Office"? The word *office* comes from the Latin word *opus*, or "work." For the early church, the Daily Office—praying at fixed times throughout the day—was always the first "work of God" to be done. Nothing was to interfere with that priority.
>
> But this practice of fixed-hour prayer is one that actually long predates the early church. Three thousand years ago, King David practiced set times of prayer seven times a day (Psalm 119:164). The prophet Daniel prayed three times a day (Daniel 6:10). Devout Jews in Jesus's time prayed at morning, afternoon, and evening. Such set times of prayer were one of the Israelites' great spiritual and cultural treasures, a practical way to keep their lives centered on loving God at all times. Even after the resurrection, Jesus's disciples continued to pray at certain hours of the day (Acts 3:1; 10:2–23).[2]

What do you think prioritizing the Daily Office in your life could do over a week's, month's, or year's time? Setting aside time in the morning or evening or both to read the Word, sit in solitude, reflect, and pray would actually change your life.

Intentionality Can Change Everything

Some mornings I nail it with purposeful solitude, getting up early before our four children invade our bed; other mornings our kids are our alarm clock with endless snuggles until we absolutely *have* to get ready for the day. Truth be told, some seasons I am weary and tired and just sleep in.

Because life is full of excuses, my husband and I have learned the art of intentionality, which is not always sexy but *is* life changing. We are intentional about date nights, quality time with each of our children, meetings we need to set up, vacation and times of rest as a family, and even our spiritual formation. My husband often says, "When builders are laying the foundation of your new house, you don't just want them to 'go with the flow'; you want some planning and intentionality taking place." I would go so far as to say that it's the same with our times of reflection, solitude, and discipline. When we are intentional and disciplined in matters of the will—such as eating, working out, relationships, reading the Word, prayer, and so on—we are changed in many ways. I've found that when results don't come fast enough, we tend to throw in the towel and look for another way, when the truth is that good things take time.

Because I live in New York City, there is physically and spiritually a lot of noise all around. Margin is slim. No matter where we live, we have to find spaces of quiet and peace, "usual places" just like Jesus did. Purposeful solitude can be a game changer for each and every one of us if we'll let it be. Otherwise we may find ourselves operating behind man-made facades, faking it with grand performances, just to get through. Upon reflection, we'll see that Jesus never had a facade or false self. He took time in the presence of the One who refreshed His earthly body, gave Him direction, and affirmed His identity.

And the Song of the Year Goes To . . .

Let me tell you, friend, you're going to need a song in your heart. There will be seasons of deep pain, frustration, and disappointment, and in your times of solitude and reflection, you may just need a song or two or twelve to soak in.

In the year that I spoke of at the beginning of this chapter, the year in which Paul and I seemed to be navigating an endless storm with no view of the horizon in sight, "King of My Heart" was the song of the year for me. I had to remind my soul that God is good and that He would never let me down, even though people, situations, judicial systems, governmental structures, and world events do and would continue to. I'd put this song on repeat and dance around my house, laugh, cry, and work through every emotion, disappointment, and failure with my God, and you know what? He was always there—good, steady, kind, loving, and unwavering. He *is* my song.

So what about you? Are you faking it, avoiding looking at the state of your mind, heart, will, and emotions? Or are you ready to go there, cultivating the Daily Office of stillness, centering, reflection, and silence before God in purposeful solitude? There is no need for facades in His presence, and you'll find yourself following in the ways of Jesus and refusing to settle for a shallow faith as you purpose to still yourself before Him who loves every single part of you.

Making It Real

1. Do you like being alone, to your own detriment: "A man who isolates himself seeks his own desire; he rages against all wise judgment" (Prov. 18:1 NKJV)? Or are you a chronic extrovert, avoiding being alone with your thoughts and God to process because you're afraid of what you may discover in purposeful solitude? What are you trying to escape from? Write a list and choose to go there. After you do, ask Father God, Jesus, and the Holy Spirit what they have to say about the things you've been sidestepping? Is there anything to pray for? Any conversations that need to be had? Is there a passage of Scripture you need to be reminded of? Maybe it's time to replace a lie with the truth, once and for all. Write down all the goodness that comes to you from the Father's heart.
2. How can you be more intentional with your days so as to prepare to have totally unobstructed and undistracted time with God for even as little as five minutes a day, consistently? Also, maybe it's time for a "mountaintop" getaway. What can you do to plan for this?
3. Consider making a worship playlist of some sort. Compile your favorite songs that speak to you and cause you to run to the throne room instead of your fears. Play that song list as often as desired, even when you may not have time to read your Bible and journal. Maybe play it while washing the dishes and praying, driving and praying, on the subway and praying, or folding laundry and praying as worship washes over your soul.

7

Healing and Transformation in Community

> Therefore, as God's chosen people, holy and dearly loved, clothe yourselves with compassion, kindness, humility, gentleness and patience. Bear with each other and forgive one another if any of you has a grievance against someone. Forgive as the Lord forgave you. And over all these virtues put on love, which binds them all together in perfect unity.
>
> Colossians 3:12–14

I'd been down in Alabama speaking when my husband called to tell me that the doctors had found "anomalies" on his mum's brain, and they were going to run additional tests. We immediately started a prayer chain, gathering anyone who would agree in faith to pray for these anomalies to dissipate. We fervently went after a miracle. Weeks later when we got the diagnosis that it was a glioblastoma, an aggressive, inoperable brain tumor, we pulled ourselves together the best we knew how and planned the most memorable Thanksgiving and Christmas we'd ever had, soaking in every moment like it was our last while holding in tension that our God could do a miracle at any time.

At the time of the diagnosis, Greg and Jenny, Paul's parents, lived in Connecticut, a good ninety-minute to three-hour drive away, depending on traffic. Every Sunday, they drove in to serve and be a part of our Downtown Brooklyn community, the community they had helped build from the ground up when they moved to New York City in 2012. This was the community they adored and were adored by because they had become a mother and father to so many of the people there. This diagnosis affected us all. People did what they could to get up to Connecticut to bring meals, clean their house, and attend doctors' appointments with them. Groups from our worship team would go up and sing over Mum, who was a beautiful, skilled pianist and composer.

As the new year rolled around, the schlepping back and forth from Brooklyn to Connecticut was taking its toll, so Mum and Dad decided to move up the street from us to be closer to all of us. They got into one of the top cancer hospitals in the United States and had one of the best doctors in her field.

The day they moved from their house in Connecticut to their apartment in Brooklyn brought me to tears as I watched humble community in action. Here is what I posted in gratitude on March 25, 2017, to the love-in-action community we call Liberty Church.

> Mood = grateful. I'm not sure how people do life alone? I was brought to tears multiple times today at the love people showed for one another. Today our church community rallied together in ways that quite frankly overwhelm me—and this is just a snippet! I spent the night and today in the hospital with my daughter Finley, thankfully ruling out appendicitis but confirming a nasty virus that caused her a lot of pain, vomiting, and dehydration. After a night of no sleep, a couple of friends stopped by with food not to mention flowers for Finley. One of them on her way to rehearsal but made the time to bring my girl flowers!
>
> While I was at the hospital and my hubs was helping his parents, good friends came and hung out with my boys for the day, making it a total blast for them, while others dropped off dinner and met simple but meaningful needs. Meanwhile, a crew of people gave their Saturday to move my in-laws from Connecticut to a beautiful apartment up the street from our house in Brooklyn so our community can help care for and come alongside Jenny and Greg in the big season they're in while Mum battles cancer. And then it was the end of an era as my little sister (we've adopted her) Janelle was moved by another crew of people from our church to follow her dream and go to nursing school in Philly. Oh, and there was a beautiful wedding celebration taking place between one of our Liberty Brooklyn couples today as well!
>
> Oh, what a breathtaking life we live together through the highs and lows of it all. I love this city and the people who make it home. Thank you to all of you who are too many to name. You live out Acts 2:42–47 beautifully.

The picture of community surrounding and loving others in the midst of a dark and challenging season was beautiful to behold. It's biblical and even desirable yet takes intentionality to build *and* stick around for.

Our Innate Desire for True Community

Deep down we all desire community no matter how we're wired—introvert, extrovert, or a mix of the two. It *sounds* nice to do life with other people, like a Hallmark Christmas movie full of warm fuzzies, good food, nonstop mood music, and holiday cheer. In reality, it's not all that simple, *yet* we still long for meaningful and real relationships with other people and spaces where we can be fully ourselves, tearing down the facades we've built to self-protect. A place where we are accepted and loved for who we are in all our imperfections and yet still called higher and challenged to repent, forgive, and live the life we're destined for. A place where we can celebrate marriages, births, and job promotions as well as mourn death, loss, and pain—together.

This longing almost makes no sense. On the one hand, some of our most painful and wounding relationships have been in the context of community. On the other hand, some of our greatest moments have come from being in loving community in which we have found acceptance, love, healing, redemption, and restoration. So why is genuine community something we long for and at times vehemently avoid? We are created in the very image of God, sealed with His divine imprint, and the image of God in its triune nature is the very essence of community: our God is three in one. As created beings, we instinctively desire to reflect our Creator here on earth.

The following excerpt from the book *The Gospel-Centered Community* explains articulately the deep longing we have within to be in authentic relationship with others:

> The Trinity means that God himself is in community. More accurately, God is community: one God, three persons. "Before all worlds"—before any sort of human community existed—there was God, dwelling in perfect, loving harmony in his threefold being.
>
> In the biblical account of creation, this Triune God says: "Let us make man in our image" (Genesis 1:26). Human beings are made to image God, to reflect his likeness. That's why our longing for community seems so deep and primal. It's how we're made as God's image bearers.
>
> So if deep community is something we all want, if it's part of being made in God's image, then what makes it so hard to attain? What keeps us from achieving the type of meaningful human relationships that God wired us for?[1]

Great question! What does make it so hard to attain? Simply put—the fall of man. When Adam and Eve sinned in the garden, they turned away from the unending connection and communion they had with God in all of His fullness. We followed suit and stopped being bearers of His image, instead becoming self-conscious, covering ourselves, and toiling for protection. We then began to pursue our own self-interests rather than living a life connected to the very Being of love and one another.

The good news is that Jesus came to redeem all that was lost in the garden. Through His life, death, and resurrection, we are connected back to God and therefore restored to our created value and purpose. We are created for love and community. We are made to become more like Christ, and community will help us do just that, giving us ample opportunities as we rub shoulders with people who are different from us. We are constantly called to set aside our biases and assumptions and instead follow Jesus by picking up our cross daily as we listen, learn, repent, forgive, walk humbly, reconcile, and, in turn, thrive—becoming more like Him.

When we receive Jesus, we are given the gift of the Holy Spirit to lead us into all truth, and we instantly become a part of Christ's body here on earth: "Now you are the body of Christ, and each one of you is a part of it" (1 Cor. 12:27). I'm almost certain some of us would like to separate ourselves from Christ's body, the church, because of bad experiences with an imperfect human, either in leadership in the church or another member. Maybe, in your opinion, there are people out there who call themselves Christians whom you're embarrassed to be associated with. The thing is we can't separate ourselves from something that we become a part of the moment we lay down our lives and begin to follow Jesus. In an instant, we become a part of His body, His ecclesia, His community of believers on earth, whether we know it or even like it. We are all connected through community—every tribe, every tongue, and every nation on earth.

The Transformative Power of Community

An African proverb says, "If you want to go fast, go alone. If you want to go far, go together." In our isolation, we may be able to move a little faster, unencumbered by others' thoughts, ways, or tendencies. But there is something about being on a mission with a group of diverse people that changes not only us for the good but also, I believe, the world for the good. The vast church communities sprinkled across the earth are laden with the absolute power and potential to change the world for the good one person at a time, as we choose to commit to being on assignment together—one body, many different parts.

Sometimes we see community from an individualistic standpoint, valuing relationships for what they can "do for me" or how they can "meet my needs." If we remain there, we'll become leeches instead of life givers. And if we're following Jesus as the way, truth, and life in all we do, then we can't afford to stay there. When we shift from individualism to contribution, community becomes a place of transformation for *everyone* present. In turn, culture and society as a whole benefit from a company of unselfish believers, who are being changed from the inside out. We can shift culture, releasing the kingdom of heaven here on earth, but only when it has been done within us can it be seen around us. We will be reflectors of His image.

Being around others has a way of sanctifying us, making us more like Christ. *The Gospel-Centered Community* puts it this way: "The agent of sanctification is the Holy Spirit. The tool of sanctification is the truth of the Gospel. And the context of sanctification is community."[2] Sometimes we need to sit across the table from someone with a different point of view in order to be sharpened, tested, and refined. Our differences don't have to divide us; they can refine us.

The context of our sanctification in which we are renewed and made holy *is* community. It's hard to put "love one another" to the test without being around others who sometimes drive us mad, in turn providing us with ample opportunities to see how love really works. My husband and children sanctify me every single day. My church community sanctifies me in every season. Rubbing shoulders with other imperfect people on the journey will cause us to face ourselves as we come face-to-face with them.

As Paul notes, "Love *one another* with brotherly affection. Outdo one another in showing honor" (Rom. 12:10 ESV, emphasis added). When's the last time you outdid someone showing them honor, be it on social media, in public, or in private with a note, a gift, or a meal? When's the last time you loved someone like a brother or a sister and showed up for them, even when doing so was inconvenient for you? We can put love into action only when we are actually around other people.

Paul suggested to the Galatians, "Do not use your freedom as an opportunity for the flesh, but through love serve *one another*" (5:13 ESV, emphasis added). Serve one another? I'm too tired, too busy, too burned out, too ________ (fill in the blank) to serve someone else. We've all been there, using our freedom and free will to do what we want instead of serving another. The Word is clear: we are set free to serve others. Serving is an invitation to be more like Jesus.

Let's look at Queen Esther's life. She had a brief moment of amnesia regarding her position and calling while living in the palace, as *her* people were all about to be executed. She didn't want to risk her own death to save thousands, maybe millions of lives. She was swept along with the cultural royal tide, forgetting that her purpose on earth was greater than simply preserving her own life.

Maybe she became flippant, apathetic even, as she rested in her royal robes, ate her decadent meals, and slept in her cushy bed. How often do we make our faith all about us and what we can get, when there is a lost and dying world out there that we are set free to serve and love? Thank God Esther woke up to reality, risked her life, and saved a generation! Who knows what our serving one another will do to change the world?

In his letter to the Ephesians, Paul advised, "Be kind to *one another*, tenderhearted, forgiving *one another*" (4:32 ESV, emphasis added). Frequently, I'd like to throw my shoe at someone instead of choosing kindness and forgiveness. But then I *choose* to lift my eyes up off my navel and look at Jesus. Even as He died on the cross, using some of the last breath He had in His lungs, He was forgiving those who crucified Him. That's crazy! Am I supposed to follow suit when it comes to my accusers, slanderers, and those who hate me, annoy me, or get in my way? Yes. And I'll say it again, we'll get plenty of opportunities to do so in community.

In John 13, we read, "By this everyone will know that you are my disciples, if you love *one another*" (v. 35, emphasis added). Are we competing, or are we one? Are we tearing one another down or building one another up? Colossians 3:12–13 says, "So, chosen by God for this new life of love, dress in the wardrobe God picked out for you: compassion, kindness, humility, quiet strength, discipline. Be even-tempered, *content with second place*, quick to forgive an offense" (Message, emphasis added).

But I don't like coming in second place. I'd like everyone to cheer for me, see me, notice me, and applaud me, thank you very much! Yet love in its essence is about others. So let's love each other and cheer each other on. When one of us fails, we all feel it because we're not separated from each other—we are one body. When a part of the church is triumphant in taking ground and breaking barriers, so is the whole! We need one another, and as we love and cheer one another on, we show the world that we are the real deal, true disciples and followers of Jesus Christ. Godly community will become attractive to the rest of the world if we can get this right! Then our churches and places of gathering will become welcoming beacons, inviting people home.

Do we want the benefits of community, and are we willing to invest in it? There will always be a cost/benefit to being woven into true community, and the price is worth every piece of yourself that you *choose* to give. As we begin to see the power of doing life with one another, things begin to change in us and in our communities as a whole.

Word to the Wise: It's Going to Get Messy

Community is not just a buzzword; it's biblical. We've established that most of us would say we want it, have to have it, and think it sounds like the answer to most of the world's problems—until we actually experience it. It's obvious that I'm an advocate for community because it's beautiful in the good times *and* the heartache, but true community is messy, especially if you stick around for the long game and keep investing. Community flourishes when there is reciprocity in relationships that are not driven by agenda or a mindset of "me first."

Pastor Cedric C. Johnson,[3] a friend of my husband, spoke alongside Paul during an event called "Race, Justice, and Unity, a Liberty Family Conversation" that we hosted in October 2016 after a tumultuous summer and midelection season. Among many other things, he spoke about the four stages to true community developed by M. Scott Peck in his book *The Different Drum: Community Making and Peace*. Following are some of my reflections about each stage.

Stage 1: Pseudocommunity

In stage one we pretend to have open and balanced friendships, acting as if differences don't exist when they do. We find pseudocommunity in a lot of Western church culture. Most of what we do is false, disingenuous community, unless we're in some form of discipleship—with open and honoring communication—that is sharpening and challenging our predisposed belief systems. We attend church, slipping in and out of a service that suits our needs and schedule, greeting people with a "Hi, how are you?" but not really wanting them to tell us because we have enough issues and pain of our own to deal with.

When we remain at this "pretend" stage, we don't let our guard down with one another; instead, we fake it while living internally and sometimes externally isolated lives, even when others are physically in our midst. We self-protect and preserve; life is about us and no one else. In this stage, we tend to take care of our own needs, and we safeguard our established doctrines, belief systems, and biases, which we all have. We even guard our small group relationships, not letting anyone else in, to preserve what "we've built." In pseudocommunity, we don't engage in understanding the plight of someone else's life because it may be too much for our established belief systems or neatly kept lives. To be clear, this isn't how Jesus lived. There wasn't an ounce of Him that was pseudo (fake)—He was raw, real, and in connection with messy people. When we live in this state, we are settling for a shallow faith.

Stage 2: Chaos

When pseudocommunity fails to work, we begin to vent our grievances, disagreements, and differences; this is when chaos ensues. When I hear the word *chaos*, I don't get excited. Living with four kids is a constant, natural state of chaos, so to add more chaos to my plate doesn't sound fun at all.

Chaos is not something we intuitively want to embrace, but it is a part of life and is integral to building true community because at this stage we realize our differences can no longer simply be ignored. The moments, seasons, interactions, or world events that bring uninvited chaos into our lives force our guards to come down, exposing the true state of our hearts. These are the moments in which our beliefs are uncovered and confronted; it's here that disunity is seen, felt, and wrestled with. These are the times when relationships are tested and either solidified or broken down. These are the moments when our prejudices, agendas, and preconceived ideas are brought into question by someone else's point of view, and it's a vulnerable process. These interactions can cause us to search our own hearts in partnership with Father God, or they can trigger us to abort mission and go back into self-protection mode, accusing the rest of the world of insanity.

In a church setting, stage 2 either compels us to put down roots, look each other in the eye, and build together with an understanding that every life is in desperate need of God's grace because we're all on a steep learning curve in need of love and understanding *or* can cause us to leave and look elsewhere for another imperfect church. If we're not okay with a little bit of uncomfortable chaos that exposes our hearts, this cycle will most likely repeat in our lives, and church "shopping" can become as natural as picking out a pair of new shoes for the season at hand.

Chaos shakes things up, and if they can be shaken, there is probably a need for it. We serve a God whose kingdom is unshakable, and that kingdom is within our hearts. If something is falling away in the chaos and the shaking, let it go. As a result, the things that remain are solidified as our sure foundation.

Stage 3: Emptying

Stage three follows chaos. In this stage we choose to empty ourselves of the ego and pride that have been preventing us from entering into true community. To be emptied of ourselves is to live a life without agenda. God's agenda for our lives and the plight of humanity will take hold of our hearts. This stage is where we arrive at relationships in community with our lives laid down as Jesus did (Matt. 16:24–25; John 15:12–14; 1 John 3:16). We come to understand others without the insatiable need to be understood. It's nice when we are understood, but as followers of Jesus, we'll see that it wasn't His number one motive. For us to understand others requires that we engage in relationship with humility and compassion, letting others speak and be heard—truly heard. Grace is required for disagreement and conversation paired with truth *and* love. This is where we live in the grace zone. Grace for ourselves as we learn and grace for others as they learn—because we're all on a journey.

Stage 4: True Community

After working through the emptying stage, we can come to one another with complete empathy. We can embrace the light and shade and the joy and pain of life here on earth. This is where healing occurs. Remember, true community is messy. If we want the genuine article, we must embrace an uncomfortable yet rewarding adventure. To have the real thing means that we have to confront our pseudo or "fake it till you make it" tendencies and be okay with some chaos and the emptying of ourselves.

Marriage is a reflection of authentic community in the church body. It can be imperfect and at times chaotic, but I *choose* my husband every day just as he chooses me. It couldn't be truer with our neighbors, our communities, our spouses, our friends, our kids, and those we don't understand and may even disagree with. The real thing isn't always nice, neat, and organized.

> If you love those who love you, what credit is that to you? Even sinners love those who love them. And if you do good to those who are good to you, what credit is that to you? Even sinners do that. And if you lend to those from whom you expect repayment, what credit is that to you? Even sinners lend to sinners, expecting to be repaid in full. But love your enemies, do good to them, and lend to them without expecting to get anything back. Then your reward will be great, and you will be children of the Most High, because he is kind to the ungrateful and wicked. Be merciful, just as your Father is merciful. (Luke 6:32–36)

This is the gospel, the Good News. The book of Acts is just that—a collective of people who not only speak without putting their hands to anything but also *act* on and do the good work of the gospel, day in and day out.

I always come back to Acts 2 as an anchor—specifically in regard to the beauty of the church as it emerged on earth after Jesus ascended to the right hand of the Father and sent the gift of the Holy Spirit. The Christians' devotion and outright passion, coupled with tangible signs, wonders, and miracles, are compelling, calling us to more. Their hunger to learn and to be together, breaking bread, praying, and sacrificing to meet each others' needs, is inspiring. The sincerity, the joy, the favor, the salvation—they are breathtaking! This is *His* church—the fellowship of the believers.

> They devoted themselves to the apostles' teaching and to fellowship, to *the breaking of bread* and to prayer. Everyone was filled with awe at the many wonders and signs performed by the apostles. All the believers were together and had everything in common. They sold property and possessions to give to anyone who had need. Every day they continued to meet together in the temple courts. *They broke bread in their homes* and ate together with glad and sincere hearts, praising God and enjoying the favor of all the people. And the Lord added to their number daily those who were being saved. (vv. 42–47, emphasis added)

This passage mentions breaking bread twice, evoking the picture of the table—the beauty of gathering around a meal while prayer and connection take place, coupled with absolute joy to discover more of who Jesus is in our lives *together*.

I have to imagine that most of the people we read about in Acts didn't get to meet or come in contact with Jesus before He ascended to the Father. Because of this, their sheer desperation to *devote themselves* to the apostles' teaching, to connect with one another, and to dig in, learn, grow, and pray together is palpable—it was necessary for them. They needed each other. And we still need each other today—this hasn't changed.

Connection, chaos, truth, love, a good meal, and savoring life and newfound revelation all happen at the table. A desire to go out and bring others to the table happens as we discover the joy of coming together even in our differences. At the table, Jesus is the center, leveling the playing field as we empty ourselves to come and *hear* each other, *understand* each other, and lovingly *challenge* each other with *truth* and *love*. It's a place where we commune with Him and with one another. There is so much power at the table. And when we get up from the table, it's then time to put into practice what we've talked about—putting our hands to the good work of building together, loving our neighbor, speaking up against injustice, and bringing the good news of Jesus's love to all we meet.

What's Your Point of View?

What lens do you figuratively look through while reading the Bible? Are you thinking about God's community of believers as a whole and how the Word relates to and transforms the *body of Christ* to bring the kingdom of heaven to earth, or are you thinking about how the Holy Scriptures can propel *you* forward as an individual to live *your* best life? Most of the time we read the Bible for what we can personally get out of it. After all, our relationship with Jesus is personal, but it's also corporate, and we have a responsibility to be involved in personal evangelism to those in our world. So it *is* personal, but it's also for *every* person. Most of the books in the New Testament were written to a community of believers and not with a single individual in mind, although there are a few exceptions such as 1 and 2 Timothy and Titus, which Paul wrote to his younger apprentices in the faith to encourage their ministry and to give instruction to the churches he'd planted.

Soong-Chan Rah addresses how inward focused we've become in our Western church culture, pointing to the individualistic lenses with which we tend to view the Word of God and Sunday sermons.

> In a typical American church, are we taking teaching intended for the community of faith and reducing it to an application exclusively on an individual level? Our Sunday sermons emphasize how the individual can live his or her best life or how to have a purpose and direction from Scripture for his or her personal life by claiming the promises of a specific prayer for the individual. Too few Sunday sermons focus on how the community is called to respond to social problems or to reflect a corporate identity as God's people.[4]

Take Jeremiah 29:11, for example: "'For I know the plans I have for you,' declares the Lord, 'plans to prosper you and not to harm you, plans to give you hope and a future.'" How many times have you put that verse on your fridge and claimed it for yourself? How many times have you heard it preached to you as an individual to trust that God has your back? It has often been preached, written, posted, and used out of context. It was written to God's chosen people, Israel, as a whole. They were in exile, in pain and bewildered. God was reminding them as a community of people that He knew what He was doing and that He had a big-picture plan for their lives. Plans that would prevail despite what they saw with their eyes. Plans not just for an individual but also for them as an entire people. God cares about cities, nations, and people groups.

Now let's apply this in our own context. Why does getting community right even matter? Because we should be in our communities for the transformation and betterment of the very community in which God has placed us. My heart breaks at how individualistic and selfish we can be and have become. May we change our lenses, break down barriers, and walk out an uncomfortable, uncompromising faith *together*. May we read the Word of God with fresh lenses that cause us to lift up our eyes and put our hands to the good works placed before us. In turn, may we see the transformation of the city and nation we've been placed in.

Disciples Are Made in Community

When I gave my life to Jesus at nineteen, I began volunteering my time daily to help build the youth ministry I was saved in while working at a local coffee shop as a barista to make some money. I applied for a one-year internship program at the church, and to my surprise, I was accepted. I fell deeply in love with Jesus and wanted to give Him everything from day one, so I did what was right in front of me and poured my life into His church.

Part of our internship program was to read the One Year Bible together as a staff, followed by an hour of individual prayer, on the church property each morning. We'd come back together at the end of that hour and pray corporately before we started our tasks for the day. I didn't realize how integral this was in my spiritual development until years later.

I had wonderful pastors and leaders who came alongside me in that season of life to show me how to read my Bible, journal, pray, and worship. They sharpened, challenged, and encouraged me in my newfound faith. I was being made into a disciple of Jesus Christ without even knowing the terminology. My leaders were fulfilling the Great Commission: "Therefore go and make disciples of all nations, baptizing them in the name of the Father and of the Son and of the Holy Spirit, and teaching them to obey everything I have commanded you" (Matt. 28:19–20). Soon enough, I began to do the same for other young leaders with whom I came into contact. What I was taught and given, I gave away. Now, twenty-plus years later, I still have a passion for the Word of God, prayer, worship, and making disciples. It's my desire to encourage, teach, and advocate for people while releasing them to walk in their true identity and purpose in order to thrive in their lives and in their communities.

As Paul and I lead and plant churches, it's our genuine passion and deep desire that people would follow Jesus, not just in attendance but in every area of their lives. We all live in a fast-paced, instant-gratification, overstimulated society, so how does the slow burn of discipleship and journeying with Jesus work? It happens one intentional day at a time. We must ask ourselves, *Am I satisfied sitting back and being entertained and fed on Sunday without putting into practice what I've learned?* Our tendency to just sit back is usually subconscious. That's why we have to consciously ask the question, otherwise we will "overeat" at the church culture buffet and forget that we are called to be and make disciples, apprentices, and steady followers of the way, the truth, and the life that is Jesus Christ! Ask yourself, *Have I relegated my Christianity to taking a placebo on Sunday?* Remember, it's only a placebo if we don't do anything with what we've learned. In his book *A Long Obedience in the Same Direction*, Eugene Peterson says:

> It is not difficult in such a world to get a person interested in the message of the gospel; it is terrifically difficult to sustain the interest. Millions of people in our culture make decisions for Christ but there is a dreadful attrition rate. Many claim to have been born again, but the evidence for mature Christian discipleship is slim. In our kind of culture anything, even news about God, can be sold if it is packaged freshly; but when it loses its novelty, it goes on the garbage heap. There is a great market for religious experience in our world; there is little enthusiasm for the patient acquisition of virtue, little inclination to sign up for a long apprenticeship in what earlier generations of Christians called holiness.[5]

Have we forsaken this "long obedience in the same direction"? Have we forgotten that following Jesus isn't a flash in the pan or a song set that gives us heightened moments of emotion? And it is surely not done in isolation. We are *made* disciples, sanctified even, in down-to-earth, imperfect community—a community of people that we choose to keep saying yes to even when we are distracted by the next shiny new thing. Yes, the Father, Son, and Holy Spirit are the agent and mediator of our spiritual formation, but the context of our transformation is within community.

May I say something from this pastor's heart to yours? Community groups, discipleship groups, life groups, or whatever we call them in our specific church contexts are not meant to be self-help groups; they are for our spiritual formation. We become more like Christ as we rub shoulders with other flawed human beings. They are places to work out the good news of the gospel in our everyday lives. Every encounter with another imperfect person can be an opportunity for change. We are pilgrims on a journey here on earth, practicing for the real thing in eternity. Pilgrims spend their lives *going* somewhere; so *where* are you going and *whom* are you going there with? Because that changes everything. Remember, the journey lasts a lifetime, so continue to show up. You will make mistakes and so will others. Decide to keep putting one foot in front of the other, wrapped in grace, while walking out your salvation with every single breath you take.

A Final Note: Pain Isn't Your Enemy, but Isolation Can Be

Bent over the bathroom sink, I let it all out. As I wailed from deep within, all the pain, anger, and sadness lingering below the surface came out at the news I had just received. My mother-in-law was nearing the end of her life here on earth, and hearing those words caused a well of grief to spill out of me like a cascading waterfall. I purposely acknowledged my pain and chose to let it all out. I did it because I knew that I wasn't alone—I was held right there in that moment in the arms of Love. I've learned that we'll never know the Comforter unless we feel our pain and let Him into the process.

After my sob session, I proceeded to wipe my tears, blow my nose, and get on the phone to book my ticket home. I had just been with our Liberty St. Petersburg Community in Florida and had decided to extend my trip for a writing retreat. But the moment the news came from my husband about his mum, I didn't want to be isolated in a room by myself any longer. I needed to be with my family and the community of people who have become more than just neighbors and parishioners on a Sunday in New York City. These people are my people.

I came home to a warm house with beautiful kids jumping all over me, a heavyhearted husband who needed my arms around him, and a big pot of chili from some of our Liberty Church family who live up the street. That pot of chili lasted us a few nights around the table together after long visits at the hospital with Mum. We laughed, cried, and had Holy Communion together. That chili changed our lives, and not because it was so delicious (which it was) but because we were together, breaking bread (actually we broke corn chips *into* our chili). The point is, we weren't alone in a painful season because we had each other. The pain we felt wasn't our enemy, although not facing it together could have been. We each had our hard days in that season, and we held each other up when the moments called for it.

We need one another. The Holy Trinity is our example; we are formed in the image of our Creator and have a primal longing for the genuine article. It's not always easy, nor does it come neatly wrapped, but nonetheless we are transformed in the beautiful mess of community.[6]

Making It Real

1. Take a moment to consider how you feel about the idea of living life in godly community. Do you have any

hurdles or hindrances that keep you from doing life with others? What is at least one way you can practically choose to invest yourself in relationships in a deeper or greater way?

2. Think about how many individuals you allow to sharpen you, to speak into your life, and so on. Is there anyone whose challenging words you'd accept without defensiveness or offense and whose encouragement you'd genuinely take to heart? If you find that you are not able to do this with anyone, ask the Holy Spirit to search your heart for any place that you may need healing in order to move forward in this vital aspect of community.
3. Look around your community. Are there any specific individuals you can go out and love by serving them? Are there any needs in your church or local community that you can help fulfill? Perhaps this looks like venturing out of your comfort zone of people to invite someone new into your world.

8

Posting It or Living It?

> Always do what is right and not only when others are watching, so that you may please Christ as his servants by doing his will.
>
> Ephesians 6:6 TPT

July 2016. We were on vacation and only beginning to enjoy the sun kissing our translucent, New York winter skin when the news went crazy. We'd worked hard that year, gone through some big transitions, and pined for the much-needed rest. We'd hoped to unplug from ministry, pastoring, and responding to the needs of the people to take a breath and refresh. But the universe didn't care that we were on vacation, or at least the United States of America didn't.

- July 5, 2016, Baton Rouge, Louisiana—Alton Sterling was fatally shot by a police officer.
- July 6, 2016, Falcon Heights, Minnesota—Philando Castile was fatally shot by a police officer.
- July 9, 2016, Dallas, Texas—five police officers were shot and killed.

In just a matter of a week, it seemed that the United States was turned upside down, and we had only begun to wade into a tumultuous election season. Everyone was justifying their side, while the underlying racial divide that some would say doesn't exist in our nation came fiercely and unavoidably rising to the surface. This white evangelical pastor was confronted with a reality that couldn't be ignored, pushed aside, or silenced. I was broken. All the news and uproar on social media didn't just affect me personally; it affected our entire church, city, and nation. I felt deep empathy, despair, confusion, mourning, sadness, and anger. This momma bear was in a place she had never been before in regard to leadership and love.

Unfortunately, these shootings are nothing new in our nation's history—even recent history—with the deaths of Eric Garner, Tamir Rice, Michael Brown, and Walter Scott. Pastoring and living in New York City, one of the world's cultural epicenters, are already challenging, and this season of tension required that we grow and change so that we could listen, learn, serve, and lead effectively. My husband and I live in a city of diverse people who aren't afraid to speak up, and as white evangelicals, we can't afford to be indifferent when it comes to racial inequality and racial healing. Weeping and grieving, I dropped to my knees. All I knew to do in those moments was to ask *Jesus* what to do. My husband and I were desperate to know how to follow in His way, truth, and life.

For as long as I can remember, I feel atmospheres, be it of a room, a person, a city, or a nation. One of the many things that hit this deep feeler hard was the amount of emotional spewing from deep despair, sadness, confusion, and hate, and the finger-pointing and volatile conversations that hit every social media channel. In some ways, I totally understood it—emotions are real, and suppressed or ignored pain can be even more volatile—but that didn't make things any less confrontational or easier to hear. One remark aimed at us as pastors and white leaders in the church was the blanket statement thrown out several times: "Your silence is so loud." Ironically, that statement was paralyzing, causing me to want to go into my shell and hide. I felt as though it didn't really matter what I said; someone was going to be angry. Yet something needed to be said *and* done because this wasn't about me. Just because doing something would be confrontational didn't mean it shouldn't be done.

Some people left our church; others clung to community, processing and sorting out their relationships with Jesus and one another in the midst of the chaos and mess. We pastor a multiethnic church with more than fifty-eight nations represented and couldn't ignore what was happening, nor could I stay silent on the matter.

On July 6, I posted the following:

> I'm sorry. As a person with white skin—I'm sorry. I repent and apologize as a prophetic act for change. My heart breaks for the pain caused throughout the generations. I'm sorry for every life that has been senselessly lost. I am sorry for

> all of the fear that has been perpetuated like a tsunami. I am so sorry. I don't always know what to say or do, but we cannot pretend that this isn't happening. May LOVE be the glue that brings all of our lives together. Jesus, lead us and may we all follow you hand in hand in unity.

Some people praised me, others spewed hate, and still others confronted me for writing #BlackLivesMatter instead of #AllLivesMatter as if I was unaware in my line of work that every single person with breath in their lungs matters as a child of God and is on a completely equal playing field in His eyes. I couldn't get around the fact that a beautiful people group, *my* black brothers and sisters, was deeply grieving. Just as you wouldn't show up to a funeral and make a beeline to the family in mourning to tell them that everyone matters at the funeral, not just the person they lost, it wasn't the time to make sure everyone knew that *I knew* all lives mattered. Others told me not to apologize because I can't change the color of my skin and that I didn't do anything wrong. But this prophetic intercessor wanted to hug the world. And I just had to say something, so I did—but then what?

This started an onslaught of deep change within my husband and me. We sought out mentors, we invited uncomfortable conversations that caused us to grow, we decided to partner prayer with action wherever we could, we discovered what white privilege really was rather than casting it aside as something that didn't relate to us, we brought friends into our home and broke bread with them over tears and laughter, we learned about the need for corporate repentance and lament, we asked questions, and we keep on asking them. To sum it up, we decided ignorance is not bliss and posting something clever does not mean we are walking it out in our daily lives. Posting something and then *not* living it has the potential to become the height of our pharisaical faking it ways.

When someone first told me that I walked in white privilege, I had no idea what they meant. I didn't think I was racist, so why did those words sting so badly? I chose to dig deeper.

Reading *The Next Evangelicalism* was a game changer for my husband and me, as you may have gathered from its various mentions throughout this book. It combines humility and authority that speak straight to the heart, and it caused me to face myself.

Among many other topics, the book contains a chapter on racism in which Soong-Chan Rah breaks down what white privilege is.

> White privilege is the system that places white culture in American society at the center with all other cultures on the fringes. Research—into books, museums, the press, advertising, films, television, software—repeatedly shows that in Western representation whites are overwhelmingly and disproportionately predominant, have the central and elaborated roles, and above all are placed as the norm, the ordinary, the standard. . . . Privilege, therefore, is power. Privilege, when it is unnamed, holds an even greater power. . . . The power of privilege is that it can go undetected by those who are oppressed by it and even by those who have it.[1]

"America's original sin," as Rah calls it, is the fact that we live on land stolen from the Native Americans and built on the backs of slaves who had no say in the matter. "These corporate sins have left their spiritual mark on America. This original sin of racism has had significant and ongoing social and corporate implications for the church in America."[2] White Americans as a people benefit from these injustices to this day, and when this goes unnoticed, it can be dangerous, creating unsafe spaces. So what do we do? Confess corporately. "Our corporate sin of racism and our corporate life as beneficiaries of a racist system require our corporate confession. This corporate confession must be led by those with a spiritual understanding and a biblical conviction—namely, the body of Christ in America."[3] The body of Christ *is* the answer to the injustice and pain that we see. Boldness to wade into issues that matter to the heart of God can bring heaven to earth.

Many churches and faith communities have been doing justice and healing work for decades, some for more than a century. It's not a new work. Faith in many churches has always been intertwined with love of neighbor and justice and freedom for the oppressed. Some parts of the body of Christ, however, have allowed personal faith to outweigh our impact on our neighbor when it has always been both/and.

In her book *The Very Good Gospel*, Lisa Sharon Harper speaks to the good work that Charles Finney did for the evangelical faith and the abolitionist movement—the two went hand in hand.

> The slave population in the United States exploded from seven hundred thousand in 1790 to nearly four million by 1860. The impact on gospel proclamation? Charles Finney, the leading revivalist of the nineteenth century, created the altar call to give people the chance to stand up and walk forward, proclaiming that they were aligning themselves with the Kingdom of God. But citizenship in the Kingdom

> of God, Finney insisted, required allegiance to God's governance over and above any human governance, including the social, legal, and economic institution of slavery. Men and women confessed and repented of their personal sins as well as their complicity with structural evil. And when they wiped away their tears and opened their eyes, Finney thrust a pen into their hands and pointed them to sign-up sheets for the abolitionist movement. This is what it meant to be an evangelical Christian in the 1800s.[4]

My friend Phillip Attmore, dancer, choreographer, actor, and follower of Jesus, said, "The times we're living in are not a distraction from the gospel; they're an entry point for the gospel." The news cycles we're watching with our overstimulated eyes are *not* a distraction from building the church or being on mission—the messy mission is right before us. So let's put our phones down and stop *merely* posting about bringing the gospel to a lost and tormented world and instead follow Jesus right into the middle of it all and live it, whether people "like" us for it or not.

To change the injustices we see, we must not only change the narrative but also walk it out in our everyday lives.

The Good Samaritan

The stories of the good Samaritan in Luke 10:30–37 and of Jesus and the Samaritan woman at the well in John 4:1–42 show us what compassion in action looks like as Jesus breaks down what it means to love our neighbor and those who are cast aside. It's not just a hashtag; it's a way of life.

In Luke 10, in an effort to test Jesus, an expert in the law asked what he had to do to inherit eternal life. Jesus answered the question with a question in a way that tested the heart of the one asking: "What is written in the Law? . . . How do you read it?" to which the expert replied, "'Love the Lord your God with all your heart and with all your soul and with all your strength and with all your mind'; and, 'Love your neighbor as yourself'" (vv. 26–27). Jesus commended him for answering rightly, telling him that if he did this, he would live. But that wasn't enough for this rule follower—he wanted to know just *who* his neighbor was. Here's where his desire to trap Jesus backfired in his face. Rather than answer his question, Jesus told a story—a story that will grow our hearts even today (if we let it).

A poor Jewish man on his way from Jerusalem to Jericho was brutally attacked and beaten by robbers who took everything from him, leaving him on the side of the road as good as dead. Two religious men—a priest and a Levite, who by trade serve the people—crossed the road to *avoid* the dying man, *not* helping him, because the law stated they'd be unclean if they came near him. They'd run the risk of damaging their reputation by association, wasting their time, and needing to go through a cleansing period to become clean. Apparently, they had places to go and people to see that were more important than this dying man. In an audacious turn of events, a "half-breed" Samaritan, of the nation Jews detested, came to the rescue of the man on the side of the road. He not only bandaged him up and brought him to a place where he could get help but also paid to care for him long term.

> But a Samaritan, as he journeyed, came to where he was, and when he saw him, he had compassion. He went to him and bound up his wounds, pouring on oil and wine. Then he set

> him on his own animal and brought him to an inn and took care of him. (Luke 10:33–34 ESV)

Jesus's teaching that the Samaritan was the example of the Father's love here on earth frustrates the ways of law-based existence. Jesus illustrated that God's love is extended to all and that we should do likewise if we are to love our neighbor as we love ourselves, even if doing so confronts our biases or belief systems.

Think about it. Jesus is the good Samaritan in the story. He was born of a virgin and was probably talked about and slighted for His parents' story of supposed divine birth. The religious elite, for all we know, could have considered Him a bastard son or half-breed. Nonetheless, He—God in flesh—came to where we were and upon seeing us had compassion on our pain. He didn't just look at us and feel sorry for us while passing us by; He came to us, bandaged up our wounds, and then brought us into His family to take care of us. He's shown us, His followers, how to go and do likewise:

> Therefore, since we have a great high priest who has ascended into heaven, Jesus the Son of God, let us hold firmly to the faith we profess. *For we do not have a high priest who is unable to empathize with our weaknesses*, but we have one who has been tempted in every way, just as we are—yet he did not sin. Let us then approach God's throne of grace with confidence, so that we may receive mercy and find grace to help us in our time of need. (Heb. 4:14–16, emphasis added)

Maybe like me, you tend to identify with the one who had compassion and stopped. We never really see ourselves as the one who walks by, or at least we don't want to. I wonder if we can look at this story with fresh eyes? Don't you think this is a parable for those of us who build self-righteous towers around our lives, excluding ourselves with veiled pious reasons from helping our neighbor in need? We all do it, whether consciously or subconsciously. Maybe we're too busy, privileged, or on our way somewhere, running late and just can't stop. Maybe we've counted the cost of really helping people and find it's too high because it may cost us our time, our finances, or even our reputation. When we become consumed with power, self-imposed law, the need to be right, or religious obligation, we miss the heart of the Father. We walk past broken and bruised people who need to be seen and helped without even realizing it because we're missing what it looks like to daily *be* God's love in action. Whose shoes are we walking in today—the good Samaritan's or the religious elite's? Our "neighbor" is any breathing human being, without regard to nationality, political party, color of skin, or any other distinction. As the abolitionist Frederick Douglass noted, "Where justice is denied, where poverty is enforced, where ignorance prevails, and where any one class is made to feel that society is an organized conspiracy to oppress, rob and degrade them, neither persons nor property will be safe."[5]

We must change our own hearts first to be agents of change in the world around us.

Loving Our Differences

Race and class were created by humanity, not God. He created us in His image and delights in the works of His hands; therefore all of us—every single one of us—are a reflection of His glory here on earth.

One morning while praying over the church and our nation, I had a vision. Father God was standing with His back to me at a canvas, creating life with His brush. In His hands was an oversized wooden palette full of brilliant colors. Before He'd touch the canvas with his poetic brilliance, He'd mix a bit of yellow, a little bit of brown, a dab of white, and a little bit of this and that. The moment His brush hit the canvas with His eternal combination of colors, life and breath came into His work. He smiled with each stroke of the brush, delighting in His creation. Every time He'd come back to His palette, He'd mix a new combination, intentional with every choice and rejoicing in the creative process—not a mistake was made. What a beautiful vision!

When the disciples saw Jesus with the Samaritan woman at the well, they were shocked, but no one dared break the awkward silence (John 4:27). He shouldn't have been talking to her, first because she was a woman and second because she was a lowly Samaritan. Racism toward Samaritans was a hot-button issue for the Jewish people, and Jesus had no trouble wading into its scandalous waters.

After Jesus revealed that He was the Messiah, *her* Messiah (not just the Jewish people's Messiah), she ran back to the town to tell everyone to "come, see a man who told me everything I ever did" (v. 29), becoming one of the first evangelists we see in the Bible. She literally brought her town to Jesus!

Meanwhile, the disciples tried to change the subject, avoiding the awkward elephant by the well. "Hey, um . . . Rabbi. Have you eaten today?" Because talking about food fixes everything—until Jesus uses it to school you.

Jesus replied, "I have food to eat that you know nothing about" (v. 32).

Can you just picture the disciples' faces as their thoughts went wild: *Wait, what? Where does He store this so-called food we know nothing about? Who fed Him? Did that woman feed Him? Maybe it was manna from heaven and we missed it!*

Void of a verbal response from His disciples, Jesus went on:

> "My food," said Jesus, "is to do the will of him who sent me and to finish his work. Don't you have a saying, 'It's still four months until harvest'? I tell you, open your eyes and look at the fields! They are ripe for harvest. Even now the one who reaps draws a wage and harvests a crop for eternal life, so that the sower and the reaper may be glad together. Thus the saying 'One sows and another reaps' is true. I sent you to reap what you have not worked for. Others have done the hard work, and you have reaped the benefits of their labor." (vv. 34–38)

Meaning, what are you waiting for? This good news isn't just for the Jewish people; look up! *Everyone* is the harvest. Open your eyes! The time is now. This is bigger than you think. Samaritan lives matter too!

It's possible that the Samaritan woman and the townspeople were walking toward them at that moment, becoming one of the greatest sermon illustrations of all time. Which brings me to a point. Who's walking toward you? Where are you positioned and what is God bringing all around you to disturb your comfort zone? Jesus seemed to relish uncomfortable moments with His disciples. He doesn't seem to mind if we're uncomfortable with what He says and does; what matters is what we *do* with His words and actions.

Racial healing is biblical, starting with the Jews and non-Jews being reconciled as one family through the long-awaited

Messiah, Jesus Christ. All of humanity has been reconciled as "one new race of humanity" (Eph. 2:15 TPT), one family—sons and daughters of God—in all our differences and God-given identities. In God's perfect plan, the adoption of all brings healing to all.

> Yet look at you now! Everything is new! Although you were once distant and far away from God, now you have been brought delightfully close to him through the sacred blood of Jesus—you have actually been united to Christ!
>
> Our reconciling "Peace" is Jesus! He has made Jew and non-Jew one in Christ. By dying as our sacrifice, he has broken down every wall of prejudice that separated us and has now made us equal through our union with Christ. Ethnic hatred has been dissolved by the crucifixion of his precious body on the cross. The legal code that stood condemning every one of us has now been repealed by his command. His triune essence has made peace between us by starting over—forming one new race of humanity, Jews and non-Jews fused together! (vv. 13–15 TPT)

Racial healing and reconciliation are beautiful and essential. They are powerful ways to show the heart of the Father to a world that can feel like it's falling apart. We know that walking out the truth of the Scriptures is harder than simply reading it; nonetheless, I think we can all agree it's worth it.

I am new to this dialogue about racial healing, and I am no expert. There are incredible people of color who have written books we need to be reading on this topic, and I highly recommend we do so. As a pastor and lover of people and cities, I can only do my part to listen to God and do what He's asking and learn from those who have gone before me and who are already doing the work. Moving forward *together*, as *one*, is necessary. Let's be willing to dismantle the constructs that bring captivity to those in our world, just as Jesus came to fulfill the law and dismantle religious systems. Anything that puts barriers and hurdles in the way of people getting to Jesus is where He starts flipping over tables. The tables at which merchants peddled sacrifices in the temple were an obstruction for His people to have their sins atoned for, and Jesus was filled with holy rage. We should be outraged at anything that creates barriers between God's heart and humanity—not outraged just for rage's sake but with a holy anger that moves us to action and connects people to Love.

Are We Posting It or Living It?

It's easy to hide behind our quotes and memes, arguing about the color of the paint on the walls instead of the real issue, like the priest and the Levite who hid behind the law. Some brilliant, life-changing, disruptive movements for the greater good have begun on social media, but as with anything, we can be infused with an idea just enough to never take action, becoming someone who posts things without living them out. We're so overly connected electronically that we are losing the art of real human connection, from the art of conversation at the dinner table to knowing how to ask a girl out on a date—face-to-face instead of swiping right or left.

What if we put our phones and laptops down and *saw* people and, more than just saw them, did something for them, talked with them, asked what it was like to walk a mile in their shoes? What if we stopped being afraid of healthy, honoring confrontation (in person) in truth and love? What if we stopped being afraid of intimacy and the mess it can bring and had real relationships?

Ask yourself the question, *Am I actually living out what I'm posting?* The world isn't becoming less connected so we have to connect with humanity more intentionally.

What would it take for us to get our hands dirty and give someone the time we say we don't have? What if we engaged in an uncomfortable conversation on purpose? What if we let someone ruin our precious schedules or week? I've hidden behind the curtain of our modern-day religious towers on social media, posting #praying and doing almost nothing but raising awareness to what most are already aware of while potentially crippling myself and others in the process. We are more cognizant today of world events than at any other time in history. If we don't have outlets to help and love others, we'll end up gorging on toxic information and living at a stalemate, when following Jesus is meant to be active.

I realized in the summer of 2016 that empathy, prayer, and compassion are a great start, but they're not necessarily enough. It is good to empathize, try to understand, and share the feelings of one another, but we can't stop there. Trust me, all I wanted to do in July of 2016, actually all of 2016, was sit in a ball of empathy and never face the world again because it was *forcing* me to grow, and it was hard. Moving from compassion to action meant having difficult conversations, learning things I wish weren't true, and then standing up to act, keeping Jesus in the middle of it all. Jesus's hands were messy and His feet took Him to difficult and controversial places, which angered the religious leaders. Let's start with empathy and then be *moved* by compassion as Jesus was.

Compassion is a compound word meaning "with [com] great love and pity [passion]." The Greek word for compassion used in the New Testament is *splagchnizomai*, meaning "to be moved as to one's bowels, hence to be moved with compassion, have compassion (for the bowels were thought to be the seat of love and pity)."[6] I often feel it in my gut when I am moved with grief, sorrow, heartache, pain, or sympathy for another's plight in life. But stopping there easily turns into ulcers and anxiety! Jesus was *moved with compassion*, did something with it, *and* sent workers out into the "field" to meet the needs of the people:

> Jesus had compassion on them and touched their eyes. Immediately they received their sight and followed him. (Matt. 20:34)

> Jesus went through all the towns and villages, teaching in their synagogues, proclaiming the good news of the kingdom and healing every disease and sickness. When he saw the crowds, he had compassion on them, because they were harassed and helpless, like sheep without a shepherd. Then he said to his disciples, "The harvest is plentiful but the workers are few. Ask the Lord of the harvest, therefore, to send out workers into his harvest field." (Matt. 9:35–38)

If you're alive, breathing, and following Jesus today, you are the workers—not your pastor or a podcast—you!

A Little Advice (Take It or Leave It)

Apparently, I'm an Xennial—ever heard of it? It's a "microgeneration" born between 1977 and 1983, bridging the gap between Generation X and the millennial. This generation is said to possess both Gen X cynicism and millennial optimism and drive. I'd say the shoe fits. I spent my childhood largely without computers or the internet but came of age during the dot-com bubble. I remember my mom purchasing dot-com domains back in the day on our family's enormous shared computer. I remember life before email addresses, personal computers, or the need for a cell phone. I got my first email address at eighteen years old (thank you, yahoo.com), and I'm pretty sure I checked it once a week on our shared home computer with its massive monitor, probably while instant messaging someone on MSN. The first cell phone I ever had was when I moved to Australia and started Bible college at twenty-two. And then came MySpace, introducing the world (at least my world) to social media, and it just keeps rolling on. Now, almost everyone in Western culture has a cell phone, probably a personal laptop, and a tablet in some form, each laden with different social media platforms.

I'm an old soul who could easily unplug and live without social media. Therefore, from someone who has lived in both worlds—one without personal electronics and social media to a world consumed with them—I want to give some food for thought as a follower of Jesus when it comes to social media. Before we hit the share button, because we all know that our "platforms" can be used for good or for harm, it's good to remember that *we* are empowered to decide how best to use it with wisdom. As I stated before, social media *has* been used for good, starting various movements that have saved and changed lives. I am by no means against it; I'm simply about channeling it to bring the kingdom of heaven to earth in some way, shape, or form. I hope this advice causes us to ask ourselves, *Are we just posting it or actually living it?*

Is it a private conversation or for public consumption?

Although our public verbal process may be helping us, have we stopped to think that it could be hurting or confusing others as we pull them into our tornado of emotions and deep thoughts? Maybe you're on a personal journey with God and should think about keeping it that way. Does the world need to know your angst, anger, and process?

Is it a rant? A bandwagon you hope others will jump on? Are you tearing others down, or the church, which you are a part of like it or not, while building your own platform? Are you in the middle of a huge life transformation that needs a bit more marinating before you post about it? Is it actually helping others or leading them astray?

I'm aware that posting what we feel, think, and are doing at the moment is totally the norm—almost as normal as breathing. But as followers of the Way, we aren't relegated to cultural norms; we live a different way—Jesus's way. Perhaps I'm showing my age here, but can we stop before hitting share and let wisdom reign and ask ourselves, *Is it a private conversation or for public consumption? Will this help or hurt?*

Am I reacting or responding?

My husband and I have gotten into disagreements over things I've wanted to reactively post on social media. I often bounce thoughts off him, knowing that I have a tendency to emotionally react when I know it takes self-control to respond. I'll send my blog posts to a handful of people with differing viewpoints before publishing them when they have the potential to cause confusion or misunderstanding. I'm aware that I'm responsible for every word that flows out of my mouth and that I'll have to answer for every single one of them—the helpful, the hurtful, and the ones that lead people astray.

On top of this, when we're alone with our thoughts for too long, we may just sound smarter and more right to ourselves than we actually are: "Do you see a man wise in his own eyes? There is more hope for a fool than for him" (Prov. 26:12 NKJV).

It's easy to rant and rave (guilty!), but if we're unrighteously angry, need to be right, or prideful, those "following" us may not swallow the pill we're offering. It's easy to fall into pride and arrogance, which *can* parade around deceptively as God's grace and justice. A bit of truth mixed with love, grace, and a big dose of humility will open the hearts and ears of our hearers, who may need what we've got to offer, *especially* if we're living it.

Also, whom do we allow close enough to challenge *us*? Remember, "A man who isolates himself seeks his own desire; he rages against all wise judgment. A fool has no delight in understanding, but in expressing his own heart" (Prov. 18:1–2 NKJV). The last thing I want to do is live as an island unto myself, raging against all wise judgment and having no delight in understanding but instead listening to the sound of my own voice bubbling out of the overflow of my heart and into my social media feed without accountability.

Is it educational, inspirational, or detrimental?

I have many friends and mentors from afar whom I learn from because the moment we stop learning, we stop growing; learning is an ongoing, lifelong process.

I am extremely grateful for people who open my eyes to any ignorance, bias, or prejudice I may be walking in. I am grateful to others who study the Word deeply and see it in the context in which it was written and who enlighten me to view things in a way I never have before. I love those who can put words together that inspire my heart to action. At the same time, I've been harmed or confused by words others have written or posted. Thank goodness I have the Holy Spirit leading me into all truth when I'm thrown into confusion or disheartened by someone's words. The truth is my heart is ultimately my responsibility.

My advice here would be to pause and ask yourself, *Will this educate and/or inspire people?* Posting something educational is not always inspirational; the two don't necessarily go hand in hand. Sometimes being educated on something is uncomfortable, and that's okay. I have many friends who post "uncomfortable truth," and when it's with the hope of humbly educating others toward action, it has the potential to be transformative and helpful (depending on how the hearer receives it) and not detrimental and harmful.

Am I living it or simply posting about it?

If we all did what we posted about, or rather than posting it just went out and did it—myself included—the world would be a different place. There is a hilarious (close to the bone) video on YouTube called "Christian Girl Instagram" about a girl getting the perfect shot of her quiet time to post on social media, and one of the tongue-in-cheek lines rings a little too true: "After all, what's the point of having devotions if no one knows about it?"[7]

Let's be about our Father's business and not just post about it. Let's go out and actually love somebody with action instead of self-righteously pointing a finger at all the people we're judging for not loving the way we love—not that any of us have ever done that.

Social media has given all of us a platform of sorts—a place of leadership in our circles of influence. What are we going to do with it? Will we use it for good? For harm? For unity? For faith or fear? To bless or curse? To rally or divide? To cause disturbances in the name of "flipping over tables" like Jesus did, even though we may just be angry and justifying ourselves? If a table needs to be flipped over to bring disruption for the greater good and a change in culture, I'm all for it. But let's check our hearts and pause for a moment before we hit Share.

Parker Palmer, an educator-activist for leadership and social change, said:

> Everyone who draws breath "takes the lead" many times a day. We lead with actions that range from a smile to a frown; with words that range from blessing to curse; with decisions that range from faithful to fearful. . . . When I resist thinking of myself as a leader, it is neither because of modesty nor a clear-eyed look at the reality of my life. . . . I am responsible for my impact on the world whether I acknowledge it or not.
>
> So what does it take to qualify as a leader? Being human and being here. As long as I am here, doing whatever I am doing, I am leading, for better or for worse. And if I may say so, so are you.[8]

What Everyday Love and Justice Look Like—Ashley's Story

What if we put our phones down and were present to what was going on around us? A lot of the things we post about or bandwagons we are on would unfold naturally before our eyes. How do we integrate our beliefs of equality, love, and justice into our everyday lives? How do we live them out instead of just posting our ideals about them? Ashley is a good friend and advocate with a heart for justice who simply and powerfully walks the walk day in and day out. Here is some of her story taken from a post she wrote for our church:

> I've worked in the justice field for almost a decade, and we have a little phrase we use: Organized Chaos. We plan; we prepare; we execute. And no matter how much we plan and prepare, things don't go as planned. Why? Because people are involved, and we're all a bit complicated. (If you don't think you are, just spend some time with somebody who isn't like you, and you'll learn how high maintenance and complicated you really are.) Also, awesome things happen that interrupt our plans, and thank God.
>
> A friend of mine took her kiddos to the park and noticed another mama. She felt prompted to strike up a conversation with her, and they connected. She learned that the mom, who had a two-year-old son, was taking him to the park for the last time, because she had planned to commit suicide that day, due to the difficulties she was facing. Because my friend was willing to be interrupted and not ruled by her full-time job, her three kids, their nap times, and her busy schedule, the incredible young woman not only made the decision to live but is now growing, thriving and rebuilding her life. And they are still friends.
>
> We need each other. And if we can lift our eyes and start to see the world around us, we will be more willing to embrace the chaos. Life's just messy, and not much goes according to plan. And there's not a thing in the world wrong with that. I'm a wife, and a mom with a job, and most days, there's

spit-up on my shirt, and ketchup on my back from my son's hugs, and my hair is usually in a Mom Bun, but I'm loved, I am loving, and I will choose to focus on what I can do. Not what I can't.

Nothing has been a greater catalyst to my healing and freedom than serving others. In fact, when I catch myself complaining, I think of people who are living a great life on less, and it encourages me to dig deeper. Can we be men and women who love the heck out of people? Maybe it's another mom or dad at the park, or an employee on our team, or someone who is currently incarcerated, or a single mom we can become friends with, or a family at our kid's school.

We don't serve people because we feel sorry for them. That is disempowering, and it makes our serving about us, not about them. None of us are superior or inferior to anyone else. The ground is level at the foot of the cross. Regardless of our economic and social status, skin color, size, culture, or our need, we are called to serve and love others, without deciding if they deserve it first. No matter how small our contribution may feel, it matters. When you show up, it's significant.

"Keep open house; be generous with your lives. By opening up to others, you'll prompt people to open up with God, this generous Father in heaven" (Matt. 5:16 Message).[9]

Love in Action

Love is a noun and a verb, a person—God—and an action. I don't just tell my children I love them and hope they believe me; I show it in all the ways that speak love to them—showing up for their games, performances, field trips, and classroom activities and spending quality time with each of them. Holding them as they cry, praying for them, laughing at their jokes, being interested in their interests—this means love to them.

Romans 12:9–16 states very clearly what love in action looks like:

> Love must be sincere. Hate what is evil; cling to what is good. Be devoted to one another in love. Honor one another above yourselves. Never be lacking in zeal, but keep your spiritual fervor, serving the Lord. Be joyful in hope, patient in affliction, faithful in prayer. Share with the Lord's people who are in need. Practice hospitality. Bless those who persecute you; bless and do not curse. Rejoice with those who rejoice; mourn with those who mourn. Live in harmony with one another.

When one of my children falls off a bike, I don't shout orders to get up and get over it, and I don't ignore their pain. I can almost feel their pain, so I scoop them up in my arms and hold them until peace returns and bandages are applied.

I think we as a society are better at rejoicing with those who rejoice than we are at mourning with those who mourn. I mean, who doesn't love a wedding or a really good party? But mourning is deeply personal and takes up our emotional energy. True love in action asks of us to do both as followers of Jesus—rejoicing *and* mourning. There is nothing to be afraid of in acknowledging someone's pain—even if you don't fully understand it. We are a body, a family, and families do their best to remove their scratched lenses and love hard because love is a verb *and* a noun. If you're alive today, you were born on purpose, in these confrontational times, to be the hands and feet of Jesus on earth. Let's grieve and mourn with each other. Let's rejoice when it's time to rejoice. Let's be devoted to one another in love and honor one another above ourselves.

Jennifer Toledo, senior pastor of Expression 58, said at a speaking engagement: "Justice is the restoration of every violation of love." Pause and think about that for a moment. Let it really sink in. How can you bring Jesus's restoration and love to your "neighbor" today, while resisting the desire to post about it and tell the world of the good deed you've just done?

People matter. Every face matters in the sight of God. May we live out an inconvenient faith as humble sojourners, ever learning and understanding while serving and loving others along the way.

Making It Real

1. Do you tend to crawl into a hole, react, or pause and take a moment to respond in times of heightened emotions and major world events? What does it look like for you and your unique personality to follow Jesus in the times we're living in?
2. What did you think of the story of the good Samaritan? Where do you see yourself in the story? Be honest. What is one thing you can do today to make changes in order to see, love, *and* help others in need? What hinders you from *seeing* people and understanding the pain of others? Is it busyness, pride, or fear of what it may confront in your belief systems, or are you too trapped in your own pain to see the pain of others?
3. Do you see yourself as a leader? As someone who can make a difference in your world? Ponder again Parker

Palmer's quote for a moment. How does this quote make you feel? What does it challenge in you? How can it propel you into action? Consider thinking of one thing you can start doing today to consistently make love a verb in your life. Stop to consider the people around you who may need you more in this season, for whom you can lay down your life, or at least your phone.

9

Reconciled Reconcilers

> And God has made all things new, and reconciled us to himself, and given us the ministry of reconciling others to God.
>
> 2 Corinthians 5:18 TPT

It was April Fool's Day of the year 2000, yes Y2K. All the power was still on—Armageddon hadn't happened (except the classic movie in 1998), and life was good.

I can't remember if it was Billy Idol or Depeche Mode, but we belted out every word, laughing hysterically and dancing like fools. I'd been saved only a couple of short years when I met Tanya. She had the cutest pixie haircut with short, blunt bangs accompanied by 1940s horn-rimmed black glasses and was dressed to the nines in rockabilly attire. We'd both happened upon a friend's birthday BBQ, and we totally hit it off, laughing, eating, and singing '80s music together.

I had to leave the party early for worship rehearsal for our youth gathering that night at church. Tanya looked disappointed that I was leaving her to sing the Bangles all alone, so I invited her to come along. To my surprise, she showed up an hour early and sat in the front row wide eyed with wonder, smiling and listening to every song as we prepared for the night. After the gathering, she came over to our house to hang out, eat ice cream, and talk into the early hours of the morning.

From that day on, she was at my house almost every day, showing up after work and often sleeping over. Ravenous for truth, she asked our entire family countless questions about Jesus before she decided to follow Him. A month into knowing one another, she was out in the garage talking to my pops about Jesus. He walked into the living room with her, telling us that she wanted to become a Christian and be baptized in the Holy Spirit. We all surrounded her to pray and lay hands on her, opening the door to Jesus. Immediately, she hit the floor, saying, "I'm on fire, I'm on fire. Why am I on fire? What's happening?" Good fire, not bad fire, in case you were wondering! In an instant, everything changed. From that day forward, she has been passionately following Jesus through every high and low of her life.

Throughout our eighteen-year friendship, we've lived close by each other in Spokane, Washington; Sydney, Australia; and New York City, continually doing life together. Our friendship has lasted and been strengthened through thick and thin, but it had its biggest and most painful test in 2017.

I mentioned earlier that our church had been through some transitions in leadership over a two-year period—the right changes, yet difficult and strenuous both emotionally and physically. In the midst of each change, the enemy was on the lookout to sow division, mistrust, and destruction in the church and consequently the relationships involved. I'm only half joking when I say that I handed in my resignation letter to my husband at least once a month, with a ridiculous fantasy to buy a farm, harvest my own vegetables, and never again talk to a soul besides my own children . . . and husband if he decided to come along. I digress. The truth is that two-year period nearly took me out.

In that same season, Tanya had come alongside me as a volunteer leader to help with several things, on her own time since she also had a full-time job. My checklist was getting more and more burdensome, and I wasn't managing stress well. I was releasing my first book and writing the book you hold in your hands, pastoring a multisite church alongside my husband, leading a growing women's movement, traveling and speaking, and being present as a wife, mom, and friend.

In previous years, I had broken out in shingles or found myself bedridden due to mismanaged stress, and I didn't want to find myself there again. I came to the conclusion that, at least for a time, I had the margin for only one day a week in the church office so I could focus and write and still be a healthy momma, wife, and human being. I made several tactical moves to make this possible, including shifting Tanya's volunteer responsibilities over to a staff member whom I could meet with face-to-face on my *one* day in the office for efficiency's sake. Little did I know that the enemy would use this change to bring destruction to our friendship.

Things got weird.

It's a long story, but I *knew* I'd hurt her, and that was the worst part for me. I had brought pain to someone I loved and couldn't take it back. The damage was done, and I had to figure out how to reconcile. For a little while, I gave her space, knowing that she needed to process, even though I desperately wanted to bulldoze through her boundaries and show up at the foot of her bed in the early hours of the morning to have an honest conversation. The space between us became the devil's playground to sow lies that were growing into prickly, damaging weeds of offense by the minute.

In her own words, Tanya felt "unappreciated, ignored, used, and hurt." She believed the lie that "Andi has no reason for you to be in her life. You have nothing in common, and she absolutely doesn't need you. She's got new best friends who are better than you, and you can back that up by never being able to hang out with her." What's interesting is that the devil was trying to hit two birds with one stone here, because I also felt used and misunderstood. I was working through hurt from previous female friendships that had broken down, and I was in shock that my longest-running close friendship was on the rocks. I started to believe the lie that I was a horrible friend, unable to build long-lasting relationships with women. I was tempted to isolate myself and keep my friendships shallow, but that's not the way Jesus did relationships.

People saw the distance between us and asked Tanya why she hadn't left our church since she had a right to—whatever that means. Later, when we spoke, she told me she stayed because she knew where she was called, and it wasn't somewhere else. So she chose to persevere and hold on to hope.

Ask either of us and we'd say it was awkward, hard, trying, tedious, and painful. The only thing I knew to do was search my heart: "Every morning I lay out the pieces of my life on the altar and wait for your fire to fall upon my heart" (Ps. 5:3 TPT). I had to trust God for reconciliation while I let Him search and heal my heart.

One worship night, months later, everything changed.

I'd been walking around the room praying for people throughout the worship service when I found myself next to Tanya. We hadn't talked in months and even childishly avoided eye contact in public spaces—yet there I was standing right next to her. I don't remember what the person leading the service said except "raise your hands if this is you." Tanya's hands shot up, and she had tears in her eyes. I heard a simple nudge from heaven whispering, "Yup." Meaning, "Girl, pray for her."

I laid my hands on her shoulders, and we both burst into tears, hugging each other and both saying sorry over and over again. The chorus being sung at that moment was "Nothing here is broken, nothing here is missing, and all I see is healing."[1] In God's reconciling presence, nothing was broken or missing and healing was available. Few words needed to be spoken, just "I'm sorry" as our hearts were rendered tender in the presence of our God. I loved that the next song included the lyrics "My heart burns for you" by Delirious?,[2] whose music came on the scene when Tanya and I had just started following Jesus. It was the soundtrack of the beginnings of our relationship with Jesus and our friendship with each other. And just like that, with a song, God brought us back to His heart. The band was back together.

The process was hard, but we are both so thankful that we were able to reconcile. It wasn't long after that night that Tanya stayed at our house for a period of time, helping us walk through the illness and death of Paul's mum. She was there every day—at our home, with our kids, at hospice as a silent presence—being a friend in our darkest hour and doing whatever was needed. We sat around the table together at Thanksgiving, clearly grateful for so many things—reconciliation and friendship being two of them.

The opposite of reconciliation is bleak: alienation, chastisement, condemnation, estrangement, offense, penalty, punishment, reprobation, retribution, vengeance, and wrath.[3] We've all felt the pain of not being reconciled to God or to one another, and the enemy likes it that way.

Think about the ways Satan has sown division, destruction, and discord in your personal life, in the church, and on an even bigger scale among the nations. Since the fall of man, Satan has been working hard to get us to take our eyes off God and His righteousness and put them on ourselves instead. If he can, he'll persuade us to turn against one another. When we look to ourselves, we tend toward self-preservation and self-absorption rather than love, truth, reconciliation, and genuine relationship. We first learn what sincere love is in relationship with God, and then we begin to reflect His likeness here on earth. God sent His Son Jesus to reconcile our hearts back to Him, and it is to the glory of God when we reconcile with one another.

But How Do We Reconcile?

How did Tanya and I do it? Repent, forgive, reconcile, repeat. Easier said than done, yet divine reconciliation is heaven displayed on earth. The cleaner I get inside my heart, the clearer I see. To stay happily married, my husband and I willingly repent of our sin and pride while taking responsibility for our own hearts. We then *choose* to forgive each other as many times as it takes each day, bringing about reconciliation. This is simply and powerfully how we stay in godly community—reciprocated relationships and life-giving purpose with Jesus as our great reconciler.

The apostle Paul is bold when he calls for the people of Corinth to rise to the challenge of turning to God instead of to self, be it self-preservation or selfishness, and to do it out of their holy awe of the Lord:

> Since we are those who stand in holy awe of the Lord, we make it our passion to persuade others to *turn to him*. We know that our lives are transparent before the God who knows us fully, and I hope that we are also well known to your consciences. (2 Cor. 5:11 TPT, emphasis original)

When was the last time you were in holy awe of God? So much so that nothing else mattered but Him? So much so that His desires were your desires because your life was so deeply intertwined with His? Paul says that his life is transparent not only before the Lord but also before the Corinthians, and his hope is that it's "well known" to their consciences! This is the height of repentance and transparency—nothing to prove or hide before God or others. It's a life lived leaning into God instead of leaning into our own ways. Keeping our hearts clean in such a deep and beautiful way is the first step toward reconciliation.

In the next verse, Paul says, "We're not taking an opportunity to brag, but giving you information that will enable you to be proud of us, and to answer those who esteem outward appearances while overlooking what is in the heart" (v. 12 TPT). There is pure gold. *Our hearts are our responsibility.* On the day we stand before God, we can't blame others for the state of our hearts when we are personally empowered to repent and forgive. Paul's not bragging but living pure to be an example to the church, bringing truth to a world that esteems outward appearances over the motives of the heart. Sound familiar? As I said earlier, we like to quote about reconciliation on our social channels, but actually dealing with our hearts and doing the deep work of reconciliation must be intentional. Are we posting about reconciliation or living it? We won't answer for how eloquently we spoke about repentance, forgiveness, and reconciliation; we will, however, give account for how we walked them out. Reconciliation—be it relational, spiritual, or racial—starts with the heart, as we see in the following passage:

> For it is Christ's love that fuels our passion and motivates us, because we are absolutely convinced that he has given his life for all of us. This means all died with him, so that those who live should no longer live self-absorbed lives but lives that are poured out for him—the one who died for us and now lives again. So then, from now on, we have a new perspective that refuses to evaluate people merely by their outward appearances. For that's how we once viewed the Anointed One, but no longer do we see him with limited human insight.
>
> Now, if anyone is enfolded into Christ, he has become an entirely new creation. All that is related to the old order has vanished. Behold, everything is fresh and new. And God has made all things new, and reconciled us to himself, and given

us the ministry of reconciling others to God. In other words, it was through the Anointed One that God was shepherding the world, not even keeping records of their transgressions, and he has entrusted us to the ministry of opening the door of reconciliation to God. We are ambassadors of the Anointed One who carry the message of Christ to the world, as though God were tenderly pleading with them directly through our lips. So we tenderly plead with you on Christ's behalf, "Turn back to God and be reconciled to him." (vv. 14–20 TPT)

Let's Break This Passage Down

- The motivations of our hearts and minds manifest themselves in the words of our mouths and the work of our hands. Ask yourself, *What's my prominent motivation in life? My individual needs, wants, and desires, or Christ?* (v. 14).
- We died with Jesus when we surrendered our lives to follow Him. Therefore, we should no longer live self-absorbed lives but lives poured out for Him. Ask yourself, *What am I pouring my life out for?* Be honest with yourself (v. 15).
- Ask yourself, *How do I view humanity? Through a lens of limited human insight or through God's eyes?* If we are living poured-out lives for Christ, with Him as our motivation, then our view of humanity should be changing on a daily basis. Do you view/judge people, consciously or unconsciously, by their sins, race, political preferences, class, job, standards of earthly beauty, weight, nationality, bias, personal values or standards, and so on? Or do you view them as created beings with value beyond measure because they carry the literal imprint of

God? Reconciliation is very difficult when we view one another through a broken lens—every soul alive today is on a journey and in process. We will never take the first step if we don't ask God for His point of view (v. 16).

- Ask yourself, *Do I live entangled in the "old order" of my life—the ways that used to be familiar to me? Or do I remind myself daily that I am enfolded into Christ and therefore have become an entirely new creation?* When we live according to our old ways, reconciliation isn't even an option because we are still highly self-absorbed (whether we think we are or not). But when we allow Jesus to reconcile us to our true identity in Him, with the understanding that He has come to reconcile *all* things, we begin to walk, act, and live differently from the inside out, even in our relationships with others (v. 17).
- When we begin to understand who we are in Christ, He becomes our motivation day in and day out. We pour ourselves out for His cause in every sphere of our lives, understanding that we are connected and reconciled to God through Jesus. We are made new, and we desire this for others. Therefore, our motives begin to change and we desire to see people reconciled to God and to others in relationship. As we open the door for others to His love, do we long for them to see the Shepherd who makes all things new by not holding our transgressions or sins against us? Ask yourself, *Do I desire to see others reconciled to God, and do I desire reconciliation in my life where relationships are broken down?* (vv. 18–19).
- Earthly ambassadors represent one nation on the territory of another nation. The French Embassy in New

> York City is on 5th Avenue. When you walk through its doors, you are on French soil, even though the building itself is in New York City. In the same way, we're ambassadors for heaven here on earth. We have our feet in two nations—a spiritual nation and an earthly nation. The king of our heavenly nation is Jesus, the Anointed One, and we are ambassadors for Him here on earth. We show people what heaven on earth looks like through reconciliation. Ask yourself, *Do I live like an ambassador for the Anointed One, or am I letting others do that job because "it's not my gifting"?* According to this passage, we're all called, anointed, and gifted as ambassadors for Christ, who is reconciling the earth to Father God and reconciling us to one another (v. 20).

Reconciliation actually makes *all things* new, just like Jesus made us new when we began a life of following Him. We are first reconciled to God and then to one another.

Practical Steps to Reconciliation

We've looked at God's plan, but how do we practically do it in our everyday lives and relationships? How do we stop faking it and follow Jesus into the beauty of reconciliation? Nothing Hidden Ministries has developed a great reconciliation that my husband and I and our pastoral staff have used. Before you begin, both you and the individual you hope to reconcile with should take some time to assess any unresolved hurts between you. Then, with a sincere desire to change and do whatever is needed for reconciliation, take turns going through the following steps:

Respond to the following with clear, concise statements and without any explanation or justification for your behavior.

1. This is what I did wrong or this is what I did that hurt you.
2. This is the pain that I believe I put you through because of what I did.
   Ask for feedback ("Did I identify and understand the pain you went through?").
3. This is how I feel about putting you through that pain.
4. Express your sincere desire and intention to change this behavior and not bring this pain into the relationship in the future.
5. Look at the other person and ask them, "Can you forgive me for this pain I have brought to you or this wrong I have done to you?"[4]

Some of you may have just rolled your eyes at this process—be honest. Or maybe you thought to yourself, *Who even does this?* and that it's ridiculous to use a step-by-step reconciliation tool. You may be asking, "Okay, but really—how do I reconcile with someone?" because you'd like a different way. Well, there's no magical potion for reconciliation. If we desire to step out of the shallows and into the deep, following Jesus in a richer way, then sitting down and having a heart-to-heart conversation to bring about reconciliation is key—because He *is* the reconciler.

Reconciliation Is a Two-Way Street

What do we do if the other party doesn't want to reconcile? This may be one of the most painful things in life—others' free will. We cannot control the outcomes of someone else's choices. We may desire to repair a relationship with someone, but if the desire is not reciprocated, reconciliation is virtually impossible—in the flesh. This is where prayer comes in. Often, our first port of call is trying to work things out in the flesh, not in the spirit with prayer. When reconciliation seems impossible, God loves to step in where and when we invite Him.

It's also important to note that if the other party is dangerous—physically, mentally, or emotionally—reconciliation looks different. Walk this out in godly community with wise counsel. Reconciliation might simply look like forgiveness *in your heart* toward them so that you're reconciled to God. Then take the next step and pray for them from a distance, that they too would be reconciled in every way to God. It's possible that a solid boundary may need to remain in place, depending on the extenuating circumstances. Seeking the Holy Spirit's direction in these situations is vital.

Prayer for our "enemies" is difficult but biblical:

> You have heard that it was said, "Love your neighbor and hate your enemy." But I tell you, love your enemies and pray for those who persecute you, that you may be children of your Father in heaven. He causes his sun to rise on the evil and the good, and sends rain on the righteous and the unrighteous. If you love those who love you, what reward will you get? Are not even the tax collectors doing that? And if you greet only your own people, what are you doing more than others? Do not even pagans do that? Be perfect, therefore, as your heavenly Father is perfect. (Matt. 5:43–48)

Jesus died for the righteous and the unrighteous. He died for those who crucified Him *and* for those who followed

Him. *Everyone*, as long as they still have breath in their lungs, has a chance to be reconciled to God—from a homemaker to a criminal. We simply never know the power of our prayers.

When Jesus taught us how to pray, He said to the Father, "Your kingdom come, your will be done, on earth as it is in heaven" (Matt. 6:10), which means there is a will in heaven that can be brought here to earth, manifesting itself in our lives and the lives of those around us. Often, we don't ask God what His will is and instead think about what we want. But we ought to be praying in alignment *with* God and His desires. His will is that *all* would be reconciled to Him and that we would then be reconciled to one another. We don't have to ask Him if reconciliation is His will, because we already know it is! So when our backs are against a wall, or someone else is using their free will to deny us reconciliation, we should pray for them, specifically for healing in the relationship. Don't lose faith that it can happen, even on the darkest day.

Hard-Fought Revelation

I had this hard-fought revelation: no one owes me a *thing* because Jesus has already done *everything* for me.

When Tanya and I weren't talking, did I want her to come and apologize to me? Did I feel entitled to it in my heart and mind? One hundred percent. That's where *I* had the power to change—in *my* heart and mind, not hers. The moment we start acting like __________ [insert name] owes us something is the moment life becomes all about us. We are responsible for our hearts. Repentance and forgiveness are within our power; reconciliation has to be walked out in reciprocity. I am grateful every single day that God made the first move so that Tanya and I could *choose* to reciprocate the love He poured out for us.

When we assume things about someone else, first in our minds, then pondered in our hearts, and then usually out of our mouths, we begin to bear false witness about them. Reconciliation starts with honor—believing the best about one another. Most people are doing the best they can with what they have and know, making decisions based on what they think is the right thing to do. Start with seeing people through God's eyes before making assumptions about their motives. They are daughters and sons of God first and foremost.

I realize that some of our greatest pain comes from relationships we have no power to reconcile. However, some of our greatest triumphs come from reconciliation with someone with whom relationship had been damaged and broken. It truly is to the glory of God.

Imagine a world where every tribe and tongue are actually living as one—in harmony. Reconciled completely. That's what heaven looks like, and we are ambassadors of the Anointed One bringing heaven to earth.

Making It Real

1. Read through and highlight what stands out to you in 2 Corinthians 5. Don't just read it though—let it read you, examining your heart. Use the bullet points provided in this chapter to break down the passage as a study guide or a "heart guide," if you'd like. Take the

"ask yourself" questions and write out your answers, allowing God to search your heart.

2. Following Jesus means following Him into reconciliation. Are there relationships in your life that need to be restored? Write a list of names and pray over each one, asking the Father for direction in what to do. Do you need to call someone or reach out to get together for coffee? Do you need to keep a solid boundary in place due to an unsafe relationship but need to begin praying for them, even if it's not easy? What can you start today?
3. Is there someone you've made assumptions about and begun to bear false witness about either in your heart or to others? Take a moment to ask God to show you the way He sees them, as a son or a daughter. If you need to, repent and ask for forgiveness for making assumptions about them and their character. How can you actively honor that person today? Is it an uplifting text or email with encouragement? Maybe God is showing you the gold to be unearthed in them. How can you help speak that into existence?

10

Living toward Eternity

> The Spirit and the bride say, "Come!" And let the one who hears say, "Come!" Let the one who is thirsty come; and let the one who wishes take the free gift of the water of life.
>
> Revelation 22:17

I'd been restless all night, in and out of a dreamlike state. When I woke up in the morning, I felt as if I had been in a fistfight—and I was on the losing side. Swinging my feet over the side of the bed, I rested my elbows on my knees and set my head in my hands, eyes tightly shut, inhaling a few deep breaths and taking a moment to shake off the feeling of heaviness that I woke up with.

As I walked into the living room to go make some coffee, my youngest son, Sammy, who's a prophetic dreamer, came running toward me and said, "Mom, I had a dream last night. A snake came into my classroom at school and bit me on the foot, and then I cut off its head. My teacher wouldn't let me go to the nurse and told me I had a bad attitude. The snake bit only me, Mom, and not my friends! And my friends didn't even help me!" I scooped him up in my arms, holding him close to my heart. I asked him what he thought the dream meant and prayed protection over his powerful little life. With a sigh of gratitude, I also thanked God for speaking to me through his dream.

The serpent had snuck in while we slept, in my dreams and my son's, agitating things in me that were under the surface that I needed to face. I was angry about a handful of things and needed a breakthrough, but it wouldn't come without my seeking an eternal perspective. The warning from my son's dream was that the serpent would sneak in wherever and however he could, coming after *my* seed—the future generation—if I didn't confront certain things in my generation. It was time for me to wake up to what was at hand.

I asked my mom to come spend some time with me and walked her through what I was wrestling with. I felt vulnerable and afraid of what was coming to the surface. I'd gone into self-protection mode; anger was my shield, indicating to me something deeper.

We read Psalm 91 out loud and prayed together as I rejected the lie that I was alone in my wrestling.

> When you sit enthroned under the shadow of Shaddai, you are hidden in the strength of God Most High. He's

> the hope that holds me and the Stronghold to shelter me, the only God for me, and my great confidence. He will rescue you from every hidden trap of the enemy, and will protect you from false accusation and any deadly curse. His massive arms are wrapped around you, protecting you. You can run under his covering of majesty and hide. His arms of faithfulness are a shield keeping you from harm. (vv. 1–4 TPT)

I broke agreement with what I feared and instead leaned into eternity—into truth, love, and my God, who never, ever forsakes me.

Mom reminded me that this is faith in action in our following of Jesus: a day-in, day-out choice of leaning into the eternal and living in such a way that our lives here on earth align with our divine inheritance. She reminded me that following Jesus is more than quoting our favorite Scripture passages as if they were Band-Aids for our problems; it's a trust that every Word of God is true, deeply healing, and transformative. Living toward eternity is a life of beautiful, uncompromising surrender. We, the bride, are being perfected every day, *if* we so choose.

In his book *Preparing for Heaven*, Gary Black says:

> The bride of Christ is being perfected. Every wrinkle and spot is being removed. It is in our relational dynamics where this cleaning and pressing must be most intensely focused. God will make this come to pass. The question is when, not if. We should ask ourselves if we are willing to be straightened out in regard to our relationships. Am I willing to have my spotted bruises exposed to God's light and love? Am I willing to recognize the damage I have inflicted on

> others, to come under the conviction of the Holy Spirit's guidance regarding my fears, blaming, and isolation so that I can learn how to live in harmony and unity with those in my life who are most near and dear to me and to God? If I'm not, I must ask why. . . . Jesus's prayer in John 17 is amazing, mysterious, and beautiful in the depth of relationship it describes. Can I endure such intimacy? Do I long to know and be known by others? Do I want to? My relationships on earth will provide all the evidence I need to determine that answer. It's ironic to consider that our preparation for heaven should be marked by relationships on earth so significant, rich, and fulfilling that we are torn by the unsolvable dilemma of wanting to stay in the comfort of our loving relations here while longing to rekindle and start new relationships that lie in waiting. Is that how you live your life now?[1]

We're invited daily to be continually perfected in Christ. Do we really want it, or are we content to cruise (which is also faking it), and if we are "content" in a harmful, detrimental sense, what does that tell us about what we're leaning into? This earth will fade away, but eternity never will, so we must ask ourselves, *What are we living for? What are we preparing for?* There are more facets of Christ to discover, more of the mystery and majesty of God to find, like hidden treasure, and the Holy Spirit is our gift and guide on this pilgrimage of faith and encounter.

In Pursuit

I ask myself often, *Am I really hungry for the bread of life? Am I thirsty for living water? Or am I content in the shallows, satiating my thirst and hunger with things that don't fully satisfy?* Don't get me wrong. We are meant to enjoy the things of this world—I mean, food is my favorite—but not at the expense of our relationship with the divine. Do I want to merely slide into heaven and live as I please while still on earth? If that *is* the case, have I truly encountered the real and living God? Am I faking it, or am I a passionate follower of Jesus Christ, in pursuit of all that He has for me, living fully alive?

A. W. Tozer says in his book *The Pursuit of God*:

> Before a sinful man can think a right thought of God, there must have been a work of enlightenment done within him; it may be imperfect, but it is a true work nonetheless, and is the secret cause of all desiring and seeking and praying which may follow. . . . The impulse to pursue God originates with God, but the outworking of that impulse is our following hard after Him; and all the time we are pursuing Him we are already in His hand: *Thy right hand has upheld me.*[2]

When I encountered Jesus at nineteen, I wanted nothing more than to absorb, learn, taste, see, and follow *hard* after Him. Owning my life ended then and there—willingly. Happily, even. My journey thus far has been full of imperfections, blunders, tragedy, routine, trauma, discipline, joy, and triumph, and in it all, God is everything to me.

The Book of Revelation

The Gospels—Matthew, Mark, Luke, and John—reveal to us who Jesus was and how He lived, telling the story of

His birth, life, death, and resurrection. They are life to our bones and mirrors to our hearts, giving direction in how to follow Jesus in all His ways. The book of Revelation is a continuation of the Gospels, the unveiling of the glory of Jesus Christ, not as God the man who walked the earth but as the King of Kings and Lord of Lords after His resurrection and ascension.

In the Gospels, Jesus often spoke in parables, the language not of the head but of the heart. It's why we love movies, television, and theater as a society—the stories told go past our minds and speak directly to our very core. The book of Revelation is an extravagant vision given to and written by the "beloved" disciple, John, revealing Christ's resurrected nature to us if we so let it. The introduction to the book of Revelation in *The Passion Translation* says:

> Only the Holy Spirit can unveil Christ to the unbeliever, and only the Holy Spirit can unveil the glory of Christ to those who know him. The purpose of the Revelation is to unveil Christ to our hearts like no other book in the Bible. . . . Revelation was written for every church, every lover of God in every generation. It is for today! It is for you to understand and embrace as much as it was for the early churches who received John's letter of Christ's unveiling.[3]

As I read Revelation once again, the letters to the seven churches challenged me deeply as to what the Spirit is saying *now* to our hearts and to His Bride. Let's take a moment to allow the Word of God to "read us" as we look at these powerful letters and lean into the eternal. They are all promises to the ones who overcome! We can't fake this!

The Seven Churches and Our Hearts Today

Christ's Letter to Ephesus

> I know all that you've done for me—you have worked hard and persevered. I know that you don't tolerate evil. You have tested those who claimed to be apostles and proved they are not, for they were imposters. . . . *But* I have this against you: *you have abandoned the passionate love you had for me at the beginning*. Think about how far you have fallen! *Repent and do the works of love you did at first*. I will come to you and remove your lampstand from its place of influence if you do not repent. . . . The one whose heart is open let him listen carefully to what the Spirit is *saying now* to all the churches. To the one who overcomes I will give access to feast on the fruit of the Tree of Life that is found in the paradise of God." (2:1–2, 4–6, 7 TPT, emphasis added)

This is a *now* letter to the doer, aka faker, in all our hearts who is intent on keeping up appearances and following the letter of the law without seeking *true* life and without living *in* the love we first had in the beginning. Repent! And let the unsearchable love of God sink down into the depths of your heart once again. This is a gospel that goes beyond our minds and transforms our hearts and, in turn, our entire lives. Father, restore unto us the *absolute* joy of our salvation! May we stand in holy awe and wonder at Your rescuing love!

Christ's Letter to Smyrna

> I am aware of all the painful difficulties you have passed through and your financial hardships, even though, in fact, you possess rich treasure. And I am fully aware of the slander that has come against you from those who claim to be Jews

> but are really not, for they are a satanic congregation. *Do not yield to fear in the face of the suffering to come*, but be aware of this: the devil is about to have some of you thrown into prison to *test your faith*. For ten days you will have distress, but *remain faithful to the day you die* and I will give you the victor's crown of life. The one whose heart is open let him listen carefully to what the Spirit is *presently saying* to all the churches. The one who conquers will not be harmed by the second death. (2:9–11 TPT, emphasis added).

This is a *now* letter reminding us that hardships, slanderous attacks, and suffering don't mean we're failing in our faith—they're a part of life as we sojourn here on earth. It's a letter encouraging us to rise up and not yield to fear in the face of suffering that is to come. It's a call to remain faithful to God in testing and trial—until the day we breathe our last. It's a letter we'd like to hand to someone else but nonetheless speaks to us in our seasons of hardship and pain. May we be the ones who overcome!

Christ's Letter to Pergamum

> I know where you live—where Satan sits enthroned, yet you still cling faithfully to the power of my name. You did not deny your faith in me even in the days of my faithful martyr Antipas, who was executed in your city, where Satan lives. Nevertheless, *I have a few things against you*. There are some among you *who hold to the teachings* of Balaam, who taught Balek to entice the Israelites to eat things that were sacrificed to idols and to commit sexual immorality. Furthermore, you have some who hold to the doctrines of the Nicolaitans. *So repent*, then, or I will come quickly to war against them with the sword of my mouth. But the one whose heart is open

> let him listen carefully to what the Spirit is *presently saying* to all the churches. To everyone who is victorious I will let him feast on the hidden manna and give him a shining white stone. And written upon the white stone is inscribed his new name, known only to the one who receives it. (2:13–17 TPT, emphasis added)

Pergamum was the center of Roman worship, with an altar built to the Greek god Zeus. It was a city in which absolute allegiance to the emperor was demanded. This is a *now* letter to each and every one of us who has misplaced our worship, surrendering to popular culture over a life of surrender to God. Balaam taught the people to live a life of immorality and to turn to idol worship, and it seems that this had mixed into church culture. The Spirit is *presently* saying to each and every one of our hearts, repent! Instead, feast on the goodness of God, surrender your life to Him, and worship Him *only* with all that you are!

Christ's Letter to Thyatira

> I know all that you've done for me—your love and faith, your ministry and steadfast perseverance. In fact, you now excel in these virtues even more than at first. *But I have this against you*: you *tolerate* that woman Jezebel, who calls herself a prophetess and is seducing my loving servants. She is teaching that it is permissible to indulge in sexual immorality and to eat food sacrificed to idols. I have waited for her to repent from her vile immorality, but she refuses to do so. *Now I will lay her low with terrible distress along with all of her adulterous partners if they do not repent*. And I will strike down her followers with a deadly plague. *Then all the congregations will realize that I am the one who thoroughly*

> *searches the most secret thought and the innermost being. I will give to each one what their works deserve*. But to the rest of you in Thyatira who don't adhere to the teachings of Jezebel and have not been initiated into deep satanic secrets, I say to you (without laying upon you any other burden): *Cling tightly to all that you have until I appear*. To everyone who is victorious and continues to do my works to the very end I will give you authority of the nations to shepherd them with a royal scepter. And the rebellious will be shattered as clay pots—even as I also received authority from the presence of my Father. I will give the morning star to the one who experiences victory. So the one whose heart is open let him listen carefully to what the Spirit is *presently saying* to all the churches. (2:19–29 TPT, emphasis added)

This is a *now* letter to our hearts, to those of us who are loving well, have a strong faith in Christ, are ministering to others, and are persevering in the midst of it all. But it's also a warning to each of us to let go of a detrimental tolerance and compromise.

Jezebel, King Ahab's immoral wife, mixed the worship of Baal with the worship of the one true God. When we tolerate the immoral "Jezebels" in our lives or churches, we step into agreement with their power, in turn, leading others astray. This is a call to repent and turn from our partnership with and tolerance of evil spirits and immorality that have mixed in with our worship of the one true God! This letter states that we'll become aware that God is the One who thoroughly searches the most secret thoughts of our innermost being when we see that He no longer tolerates the Jezebel spirit rife with immorality, laying it low and striking it down. Let's choose to let go of a negative form of tolerance and crippling compromise before we pay the costly price of surrendering to it. We are urged to cling tightly to all that we have—to the purity of the gospel until Christ appears.

Christ's Letter to Sardis

> I know all that you do and I know that you have a reputation for being really "*alive*" but you're actually *dead*. *Wake up* and *strengthen* all that remains before it dies, for I haven't found your works to be perfect in the sight of my God. So remember all the things you've received and heard, then *turn back to God* and obey them. For if you continue to slumber, I will come to you like a thief, and you'll have no idea at what hour I will come. Yet there are still a few in Sardis who have remained pure, and they will walk in fellowship with me in brilliant light, for they are worthy. And the one who experiences victory will be dressed in white robes and I will never, no never erase your name from the Book of Life. I will acknowledge your name before my Father and his angels. So the one whose heart is open let him listen carefully to what the Spirit is *now saying* to all the churches. (3:1–6 TPT, emphasis added)

This is a *now* letter to the faker who rears its ugly head in all our hearts and deceives us into believing or thinking that we're fully alive. But if we are not aligned with the eternal, we are actually dead. I believe it's a letter to the church today whose programs, constructs, and run sheets *can* take precedence over presence and the life found in Christ, which brings true awakening to everyone. A. W. Tozer says:

> Sound Bible exposition is an imperative must in the church of the living God. Without it, no church can be a New Testament

> church in any strict meaning of the term. But exposition may be carried on in such a way as to leave the hearers devoid of any true spiritual nourishment whatsoever. For it is not mere words that nourish the soul, but God Himself; and unless and until the hearers find God in personal experience, they are not the better for having heard the truth.[4]

We're implored to be doers and not just hearers of the Word (James 1:22). This means we must read and ingest it daily, feed on it, let it read and awaken us, and then walk in the gift of unfathomable grace to see it outworked in our lives, from holiness, to miracles, to healing, to sharing the gospel, to purity, and so forth.

If you're reading these words—you're not dead yet! Wake up and strengthen all that remains! It is not too late. Repent of clinging to your ways and turn back to God in *all* your ways, acknowledging Him, and He will lead you on the path of life!

Christ's Letter to Philadelphia

> I know all that you've done. Now I have set before you a wide-open door that none can shut. For I know that you possess only a little power, yet *you've kept my word and haven't denied my name. . . . Because you've passionately kept my message of perseverance*, I will also keep you from the hour of proving that is coming to test every person on earth. But I come swiftly, so cling tightly to what you have, so that no one may seize your crown of victory. For the one who is victorious, I will make you to be a pillar in the sanctuary of my God, permanently secure. I will write on you the name of my God and the name of the city of my God—the New Jerusalem, descending from my God

> out of heaven. And I'll write my own name on you. So the one whose heart is open let him listen carefully to what the Spirit is *now saying* to all the churches. (3:8, 10–13 TPT, emphasis added)

This letter is beautiful. There is no warning or call to repentance, just affirmation that a door is wide open into the kingdom of God because the church of Philadelphia has kept the Word of God and not denied Christ, even though they "possess only a little power." Imagine what would take place if they, *or we*, walked in more of the power of God. We wouldn't just be kept from denying Christ but would also see miracles, signs, and wonders beyond measure!

Jesus exhorts the church to cling tightly to what we have so that no one may seize our crown of victory because He will come soon.

Christ's Letter to Laodicea

> I know all that you do, and I know that you are neither frozen in apathy nor fervent with passion. How I wish you were either one or the other! But because you are neither cold nor hot, but lukewarm, *I am about to spit you from my mouth*. . . . All those I dearly love I unmask and train. So *repent and be eager to pursue what is right*. Behold, I am standing at the door, knocking. If your heart is open to hear my voice and you open the door within, I will come in to you and feast with you, and you will feast with me. And to the one who conquers I will give the privilege of sitting with me on my throne, just as I conquered and sat down with my Father on his throne. The one whose heart is open let him listen carefully to what the Spirit is *saying now* to the churches. (3:15–16, 19–22 TPT, emphasis added).

This letter brought me to my knees. There have been times when I've been "lukewarm," cruising without passion, yet at the same time, not completely apathetic in my following of Jesus—and it's unsettling to admit. He's always knocking on the door of our hearts with an invitation to more—will we sit back and ignore the offer? Or will we walk in passion, opening the door to all that Christ has for us in this life and into eternity?

Go back and reread the reward for being victorious in each of these letters. Ponder what each one says; let it search your heart and bring transformation. May Christ's lamp burn in our hearts and in our churches until He returns for us!

Restoring Eden

These letters are profoundly important to the church and, therefore, our individual lives. We live in what I call the "now but not yet." Jesus has come to save us and restore all things, but the full restoration of Eden has not yet taken place; the new heaven and new earth are yet to come. Eden, however, is being restored *within us* through Jesus, and that's why, somewhere deep inside, we all have a longing for more. More life, more love, more restoration, more healing, more, more, more of all the things that bring joy and hope and love and peace. Sometimes we search for more in things that will only temporarily satisfy, and sometimes we find more as we discover unsearchable riches in the eternal living water that causes us to never thirst again.

Our daily following of Jesus is not all rainbows and unicorns—and don't we all know it! Some seasons are breathtakingly beautiful and others are hard and dark. I wrote the following words in my journal in the middle of a season of wrestling with God over a few things, a season when I wanted to quit and live a life of solitude—forever.

> Fear. The thorn in my side that the apostle Paul spoke of—this thorn is like a dark river running underneath the surface of my soul. Sometimes the waters rage and capture my attention. Other times . . . it's quiet—but seemingly always there. Always threatening to take over and pull me under and destroy my life.

The fear I felt was intense, and when I scraped the bottom of the barrel in prayer, I saw a darkness that greatly needed the light of Jesus. After I penned these words in my journal, I turned on a TV show for the kids, locked my bedroom door, put worship music on, and asked Jesus to show me my truest reality. I needed to be reminded of my kingdom inheritance because this was no way to think, feel, or live.

As I closed my eyes, instantly I saw a vision of Jesus jumping into the dark river running underneath the surface of my soul. He was laughing and swimming in its darkness in a way that mocked its overflowing death and destruction. I started to involuntarily laugh too. Every part of the river that touched Him turned to sparkling crystal, full of life and light. And then something amazing happened. He stood, stretched out His arms, threw back His head, and smiled with a joy that only the One who has overcome death could, and in that moment, the entirety of the dark river became like shimmering diamonds of light inside my soul. Jesus reminded me just who He is and how powerful and able He is to change anything. And I mean anything.

The threat of death inside my heart, soul, and mind was enough to cause me to lie hiding in my bed indefinitely, eating popcorn and dark chocolate and bingeing on Netflix. But Jesus's *joyous* mockery of the darkness within reminded me just who had my back and loved me unto His own death and triumphant resurrection. This revelation came to me out of a hunger for more, a hunger for truth, a hunger to discover more of the divine.

Leaning into Jesus with a true, steadfast, and insatiable longing for more of Him will never disappoint us.

> He is given to us like an engagement ring is given to a bride, as the first installment of what's coming! He is our hope-promise of a future inheritance which seals us until we have all of redemption's promises and experience complete freedom—all for the supreme glory and honor of God! (Eph. 1:14 TPT)

In my vision of Jesus voluntarily swimming in *my* disastrous darkness, I was reminded that He's the hope promise, sealing my life until I experience complete freedom. It was a reminder to just keep going.

When We Don't Know, We Perish

When we first moved to New York City, I had to teach my then four-, three-, and two-year-olds some street smarts. They were used to being strapped in a car seat to get to their destination, but in New York City, we were walking or taking the subway everywhere. Often, I had my two youngest in a double stroller with my eldest holding on to the handle as we walked, especially in crowded spaces. One particular day, we were walking up to Rite Aid and then over to the park, which was only a block away, so I thought I'd let them roam free without the stroller.

They were playing a game we like to play in which they run to a certain tree and then back to me. I thought this was genius preparation for a good, long afternoon nap, so I really let them go for it. Back and forth they went until Jesse, three years old, just kept running. I called his name, "Jesse, come back! Jess—come back, babe," until I realized he was going to run head-on into speeding traffic. The bloodcurdling scream that came out of the deepest part of my gut was loud enough to cause time to stand still. The entire street turned as I let out one last desperate cry to save my son's life. "JESSE!!!!!" Out of the corner of my eye I saw Michael, the crossing guard, turn to look at me and then quickly move his gaze to Jess. Michael was on the opposite side of the street and bolted across at lightning speed just in time to scoop Jesse up into his arms, a millisecond after one of his little feet had touched down on the street. No lie, as Michael swooped Jesse up, a car went speeding by—the car that would have taken my son's life.

I fell to my knees, sobbing uncontrollably. Michael marched over to me with Jesse Freedom in his arms and set him down right in front of me—eye to eye. Michael said in the most loving yet stern way, "Look what you did to your momma. Do you see that? Don't run away from your momma like that, son." Jesse clung to me and said sorry in his sweet little raspy voice. I grabbed him gently by the shoulders and held him a foot away from me, looking deeply into his gorgeous dark brown eyes. In the best way that I could to a four-, three-, and two-year-old, I explained the reality of eternity and the temporal nature of living on earth. I explained death and that mommas and daddies want to go to heaven *before* their kids do. Explaining to my babies the reality of eternity was instinctual in that moment.

I realized that neither Jesse nor any of my kids had a true understanding of eternity, and therefore running toward oncoming traffic was of no consequence in Jesse's three-year-old mind. Not because he wanted to be careless and die but because he simply wasn't aware.

Understanding and leaning into the eternal are not detrimental to our lives here on earth. "We fix our eyes not on what is seen, but on what is unseen, since what is seen is temporary, but what is unseen is eternal" (2 Cor. 4:18). There is a whole other world at work that we cannot see with the naked eye, a world that is more real than the one we have our feet set on and from which we receive our oxygen. When we don't understand, fix our eyes on, or have a vision for something greater, we dwell carelessly here on earth.

Hearing *and* Doing

As I've stated before, it's dangerous to be only hearers of the Word and not doers of it. The purpose of this entire book is not simply to engage your mind logically and practically but to point you back to the Word of God; the Holy Spirit; Jesus Christ, the Word made flesh; and your Father, who greatly loves you. And it's not *just* to point you back but, oh, that you'd become a passionate, wholehearted *follower* of Jesus Christ in *all* His ways. Many of us would prefer to read a book or sit with a friend to get their opinion or advice than find a Bible reading plan that points us back to the way, the truth, and the life we are all called to walk in. More than that, are we willing to *live* what it says?

James, Jesus's half brother, had some amazing revelations. Because he grew up with the Savior of the world, it would be good for us to listen up.

> Therefore, get rid of all moral filth and the evil that is so prevalent and humbly accept the word planted in you, which can save you. Do not merely listen to the word, and so deceive yourselves. Do what it says. Anyone who listens to the word but does not do what it says is like someone who looks at his face in a mirror and, after looking at himself, goes away and immediately forgets what he looks like. But whoever looks intently into the perfect law that gives freedom, and continues in it—not forgetting what they have heard, but doing it—they will be blessed in what they do. (James 1:21–25)

James says when the Word is planted within us and we humbly accept it, it can save our lives! If the Word is not planted within us, deception or a twisting of the truth is a probable outcome since we're not deeply rooted in it. Even Satan himself twisted the truth in the desert as he tempted Jesus, so take note! James implores us not to merely *listen* to the Word—or as I would say, be entertained by the greatest communicators and podcasts in our time—but *do* what the Word says. Let's do it, friends—live it, refuse to be simply entertained by it but get down in the trenches and take this Christian life seriously! We will be blessed when we do.

My sister-in-law Jessi Green says, "It's dangerous to learn about the kingdom and not live it." We need to know doctrine and the Word of God, but if our hearts aren't revolutionized to the point of deep transformation that affects our actions, what is the point?

Thin Places

When I wrote these words, I found myself sitting in a "thin place," the thin place between heaven and earth that is both rich and sacred. It's a place where the eternal presence of God is felt and seen in every touch, every look, every smile, every tear, and every breath. It's a place that reminds us this earth is not our home; we are made for another world.

The hospice ward in Brooklyn was peaceful and so was my mum-in-law. It felt like a delivery room to heaven—holy. We didn't know how many days she had left on earth with us, but we were making the most of every moment. Although her breathing was becoming labored, her smile was still tender and filled with delight at the sound of a familiar voice. Even when her eyes were closed, she'd whisper, "I love you" in response to a tender touch, and when words were no more—love remained. It was felt in that thin place, filled with the tangible, eternal presence of God.

As I sat in that room, writing these words and watching my father-in-law lovingly dote on his wife, stroking her hair and whispering in her ear, I was reminded once again that we are living toward eternity. We are leaning into it, inclining our hearts, lives, and ears to our truest reality. Our entire journey here on earth is preparation for the real thing. This earth is not our home; we are just passing through, hence the discomfort in our everyday lives. But what will we incline our ears to? What will we lean into—the eternal or the temporal?

In one of her last lucid moments here on earth, Jenny was trying to express her heart to us as we gathered around her hospital bed. The words weren't coming together in the way she wanted them to, and at that stage, only her heart could ponder what her brain wasn't able to get out of her mouth any longer. Laughing to herself, she said with a huge smile on her face, "Well . . . we have forever." With tears in all of our eyes, we knew by that statement that we didn't have long. She was leaning deeply toward heaven.

The truth is we *do* have forever, but how will we follow Jesus *now* here on earth? How will we practice in the temporal for our forever? How will we lean into eternity when what we see with our eyes is constantly trying to get our time and attention?

Don't wait to dig deep, ask questions, address your pain, reconcile with God and man, love well, and be deeply loved. May we find ourselves enfolded in Christ, bowing down in worship, refusing to surrender to popular opinion and culture. May we stop *just* posting things and go and live in the mess of things and lead others to the Father's heart. Now is the time to change, and today is the day to take one step in the right direction. As ancient Chinese philosopher Lao-Tzu said, "The journey of a thousand miles begins with a single step."[5] What step will you take today?

Are you thirsty and hungry for more of the One who rescued you and loves you beyond measure? There is an invitation for more.

> "Come," says the Holy Spirit and the Bride in divine duet. Let everyone who hears this duet join them in saying, "Come." Let everyone gripped with spiritual thirst say, "Come." And

> let everyone who craves the gift of living water come and drink it freely. "It is my gift to you! Come." (Rev. 22:17 TPT)

Come, step out of the shallows and into the depths of a life lived following hard after Jesus with everything you are. Tozer tells us:

> On our part, there must be positive reciprocation if this secret drawing of God is to eventuate in identifiable experience of the Divine. In the warm language of personal feeling, this is stated in the forty-second Psalm: As the hart pants after the water brooks, so does my soul pant after thee, O God. My soul thirsts for God, for the living God; when shall I come and appear before God? This is deep calling unto deep, and the longing heart will understand it.[6]

Deep is calling out to the deep in you. There is more—do you truly long for it?

This is not about doing the right things on the outside to appease a guilty conscious or "play the Christian" because, as Ravi Zacharias said, "Jesus Christ did not come to make bad people good, but to make dead people alive."[7] Are you living *fully* alive? Jesus came to give you 100 percent of Himself. Will you fake it or follow Jesus with all that you are, even when it's not easy?

Jesus began his ministry of miracles at a wedding (John 2:5–11). He told the servants to take the dirty stone water jars used for ceremonial washing, each holding from twenty to thirty gallons, and fill them with water. After the servants filled the jars, at His command, they reached in to draw out some water and out came the greatest new wine, the type of wine that is usually served first but here was saved for last.

Jesus took tasteless water and made it into new wine, the best wine. It's also what He does with our lives; it's who He is—the last and the very best. We are still waiting for the wedding day of the bride (the church) to the Bridegroom (Jesus). We are living in the "now but not yet," pressing into eternity as we wait for Eden to be fully restored in and around us. The last and best are literally yet to come. So while we wait and prepare for what is to come, what are we leaning into? The tasteless things of this world or new wine found only as we pursue the eternal?

C. S. Lewis said, "Aim at Heaven and you will get Earth 'thrown in': aim at Earth and you will get neither."[8] With each passing day, I'm more aware of how deeply I need to lean into eternity. I am more aware of my desperate need for God in every moment and imperfection in my life. I have an insatiable desire for more breakthroughs, healing, clarity, freedom, peace, restoration, and so much more. I want to live completely alive and see others awaken to live fully alive! These are longings that nothing in this world can satisfy. I am desperate to see more of the goodness of God in the land of the living all around me. So I will continue to refocus and aim my life at heaven. I will press in no matter what I feel. I choose to pursue harder, faster, and deeper. Through every season, God has been—and is—my everything. He is the steady lifter of my head, the lover of my soul when I'm lovable and unlovable, the way in which to go, the truth my thirsty soul is searching for, and the life I long to live wrapped up in one. I will continue to follow Him, putting one foot in front of the other each day until I breathe my last.

If I could give any final words to you, it would be these three: *don't give up*. I can't tell you that you won't want to, but just remember that your desire to give up at times is a spiritual battle taking place in the unseen realm that is bigger than what you are currently seeing with your earthly eyes. You matter and so does your life and purpose here on earth. You are connected to a community of people who need your story, who need you to fiercely pursue the unfathomable riches found in the Father, Son, and Holy Spirit with a fervor and a passion that may just set you on fire, consuming your entire life. Your moments touch others' moments and together weave a beautiful eternal tapestry that is the bride of Christ. This is too wonderful to behold and comprehend with our human minds.

In this divine mystery that we are enfolded in, I implore you, I exhort you, I plead with you . . . keep going! Don't give up! Fight the good fight, finish *your* race, keep the faith with an unearthly, uncommon commitment and fervor and share it with the world. *Follow Jesus, refusing to settle for a shallow or fake faith* with every breath you take, as they are the very breath of God given to you as a gift.

Making It Real

1. Which of the seven letters to the churches spoke the most to you? Why? Do you need to repent and turn from your ways and cling to "what you have" in God instead? Think about speaking to someone you trust and praying together, inviting them in to walk this journey out with you as you choose to live differently.
2. The entertainment culture has seeped into Christianity, causing us to be repeat offenders in the hearing but not

doing of the Word. Often, we will read books, listen to podcasts, go to church services and small groups, and so on—but are we doing anything with what we read, hear, see, and have been given? Are we reading the Word on our own and applying it to our everyday lives, seeing it activated and brought to life? Meditate on James 1:22 and think about the implications for your life. What needs to change?

3. Now that this book has drawn to a close, what will the next step be in your passionate pursuit of God? Perhaps this book has lit a fire in you to see or do things differently. Following Jesus is a long obedience in the same direction until you breathe your last (and don't be too hard on yourself; many mistakes will be made along the way). Write down what your *one* next step will be. Make it something you can genuinely commit to and make a discipline in your life—the kind that will bring new life, not drudgery. Maybe it's a Bible-reading plan that is doable for you. Maybe it's waking up fifteen minutes earlier to journal and pray. Maybe it's finding a community of believers. Whatever you do, don't give up; keep leaning into the eternal with all that you are.

Acknowledgments

To the woman who called me cute and entertaining—I know you meant it as a compliment, but your words caused me to face myself and, in turn, changed my life forever. Thank you.

Jana Burson—Thank you for being a catalyst in my life. Your expertise as an agent has continued to help shape and direct my book-writing journey. Your candor, encouragement, consultation, and most of all friendship mean the world.

Rebekah Guzman, my acquiring editor—Thank you for your belief in me and my voice. It is such a joy to work with you and the Baker Books team. And to the rest of Team Baker: Mark, Abby, Brittany, and Gisèle, it is a genuine pleasure to partner with you.

Jamie Chavez—Thank you for always giving it to me straight while cheering me on at the same time. Your feedback is always invaluable. Can't wait to come visit you one day, share a good meal, and "rant" together about things that matter.

Pastors Rick and Linda Sharkey, David and Monica Von, and Erin Chase—Thank you for fulfilling the Great Commission in helping to make me a disciple of Jesus Christ. Your foundational love, direction, and shaping in those early years of following Jesus changed my life. Thank you for not just loving me but also giving me the tools I needed to walk this journey out daily. Those mornings we gathered together to read the One Year Bible and to pray taught me more than you'll ever know.

Dad and Mom—Thank you for giving me that big NIV Study Bible on my eighteenth birthday. It was seed for my nineteenth year when I decidedly began to follow Jesus. It's been "old faithful" all these years—tattered, worn, and coffee stained. I also have to say thank you for consistently waking in the early hours of the morning for solitude and prayer as we kids grew up. You never told us to do what you did, but your example was caught.

Dominika—You are Wonder Woman, Mary Poppins, and a devoted disciple of Jesus Christ all wrapped into one. I've loved our conversations around this book that were fuel for the fire on days when I was distracted or discouraged. You cheered me on and then proceeded to read every word before I turned it in to my editors. Paul and I are forever grateful for your life, love, and trust—you are family.

Trish—Thank you for kicking butt, taking names, hustling hard, and loving well. This book wouldn't have gotten done without your support, organization (of all the other parts of my life), and friendship. So glad you walked into my house five years ago for Community Group, held my baby when my arms were tired, and stole, ahem "borrowed," my gray T-shirt on that rainy Tuesday. The rest is history.

Kristin—You are not only the best big sister a girl could have but also *such* a good friend. Thank you for helping me with some last-minute things I needed to get done so that this book could be sent off to print.

Ashley Abercrombie, Ronaldo Hardy, and Meghan Matt—What can I say? I really love you all. Your feedback on the "Posting It or Living It?" chapter was so valuable. I'm beyond grateful.

Tanz—Our friendship has taught me so much, *so* much. We've been refined in the fire (big wink partnered with an uncomfortable laugh) and simply keep choosing to walk this life out with Jesus together. Thank you for allowing me to share part of our story, my forever friend. I believe it will help so many.

Liberty Church—I love you. Thank you for being committed to walking out this long obedience in the same direction together. I'm excited to be old ladies and old men sitting on our stoops, agreeing, disagreeing, praying, reconciling, breaking bread, and in general just being awesome as we follow Jesus together, seeing His kingdom come here on earth as it is in heaven in and out of every season. #LetsGrowOldTogether

Dad Andrew, Pa, Greg—You are one of the most courageous men I know, and I'm honored that you're my father-in-law.

Thank you for letting me share some of Mum's story . . . *your* story. Her life has changed all our lives but none more than yours. I honor you and love you beyond measure.

Ezekiel Benjamin, Jesse Freedom, Finley Grace, and Samuel Malachi—You are our heavenly treasures sent to earth straight from the heart of God. I am *so* proud of who you are and continue to become as each day passes. May you live *from* the depths of God's great love all the days of your lives and not *for* it—no performance necessary. In the years ahead, I pray this book will find you in the very season your heart is searching for what's written in its pages. It is my love letter to you.

To my husband, Paul William Andrew—You basically wrote (and have lived) the "Love Out of Context" chapter with me—well, all the chapters. I stole many lines from your message notes and put them in this book. The cover should probably read, "By Andi Andrew, *with* Paul Andrew"—well, every book I write should say that. So thankful for our life together. I learn more about the mystery of Christ and His bride being with you than I ever knew was possible. Our marriage is a refiner's fire, a kingdom partnership, a grand adventure, and a whole lot of fun. It's worth choosing every day. I love you more than words.

To the One who has loved me without end—The lengths You've gone to in order to rescue me and lead me in the way, truth, and life are astounding. I'm so incredibly aware that I've only scratched the surface on this pilgrimage of leaning into the eternal. Thank You for Your love in and out of every season; it has been the steady, through line in my life. When all is said and done, You are what remains.

Notes

Introduction

1. See Eugene H. Peterson, *A Long Obedience in the Same Direction: Discipleship in an Instant Society* (Downers Grove, IL: InterVarsity, 1980).

Chapter 1 Refuse to Fake It

1. C. S. Lewis, *The Lion, the Witch and the Wardrobe* (New York: HarperCollins, 1950), 86.
2. Martin Smith, "I Could Sing of Your Love Forever," recorded by Delirious? on *Cutting Edge* (UK: Furious Records, 1995), CD.
3. Watchman Nee, *Christ: The Sum of All Spiritual Things* (New York: Christian Fellowship Publishers, 1973), 9.
4. C. S. Lewis, *Mere Christianity*, in *The Complete C. S. Lewis* (New York: HarperCollins, 2002), 50–51.

Chapter 3 Identity Crisis

1. Rebekah Lyons, "First data point of the night," Instagram, March 3, 2016, https://www.instagram.com/p/BChF_w0xE3z/?taken-by=rebekahlyons. Q Ideas (qideas.org) educates church and cultural leaders on their roles and opportunities to embody the gospel in public life.
2. Peter Scazzero, *Emotionally Healthy Spirituality Day by Day* (Grand Rapids: Zondervan, 2014), 40.
3. Lewis, *Mere Christianity*, 114.

4. C. S. Lewis, *The Screwtape Letters,* in *The Complete C. S. Lewis* (New York: HarperCollins, 2002), 222.

Chapter 4 Crowd Pleasers or Mountain Climbers?

1. Soong-Chan Rah, *The Next Evangelicalism: Freeing the Church from Western Cultural Captivity* (Downers Grove, IL: InterVarsity, 2009), 47.

2. Parker Green, "Sequoia National Park," Instagram, July 1, 2017, https://www.instagram.com/p/BWAduoaDhct/?taken-by=parkerrichard green.

Chapter 5 Misplaced Worship

1. Rah, *The Next Evangelicalism*, 37.

2. Bible Study Tools, s.v. "ekklesia," www.biblestudytools.com/lexi cons/greek/nas/ekklesia.html.

3. Oxford Dictionaries, s.v. "individualism," https://en.oxforddiction aries.com/definition/individualism.

4. Rah, *The Next Evangelicalism*, 36.

5. Rah, *The Next Evangelicalism*, 29–30.

Chapter 6 Introverted Extroverts

1. Dietrich Bonhoeffer, *Life Together* (New York: HarperCollins, 1954), 78.

2. Scazzero, *Emotionally Healthy Spirituality*, 11.

Chapter 7 Healing and Transformation in Community

1. Robert H. Thune and Will Walker, *The Gospel-Centered Community: Leader's Guide* (Greensboro, NC: New Growth Press, 2013), https://www.biblestudytools.com/bible-study/topical-studies/created -for-community.html.

2. Thune and Walker, *The Gospel-Centered Community.*

3. Pastor Cedric C. Johnson wrote a book titled *Race, Religion, and Resilience in the Neoliberal Age* (New York: Palgrave Macmillan, 2016).

4. Rah, *The Next Evangelicalism*, 33.

5. Peterson, *Long Obedience in the Same Direction*, 16.

6. I would be remiss if I didn't acknowledge that unhealthy, controlling community exists and is a big reason why many are put off by church.

However, involvement in healthy community is still God's plan and is out there for you to discover and contribute to.

Chapter 8 Posting It or Living It?

1. Rah, *The Next Evangelicalism*, 72.

2. Rah, *The Next Evangelicalism*, 69.

3. Rah, *The Next Evangelicalism*, 71.

4. Lisa Sharon Harper, *The Very Good Gospel: How Everything Wrong Can Be Made Right* (New York: Penguin Random House, 2016), 7.

5. Frederick Douglass, "Southern Barbarism," speech on the twenty-fourth anniversary of emancipation, Washington, DC, 1886.

6. Bible Study Tools, s.v. "splagchnizomai," www.biblestudytools.com/lexicons/greek/nas/splagchnizomai.html.

7. "Christian Girl Instagram," YouTube video, 2:59, uploaded by John B. Crist, November 18, 2014, https://www.youtube.com/watch?v=ANv1_teeb3s.

8. Parker J. Palmer, introduction to *Leading from Within: Poetry That Sustains the Courage to Lead*, by Sam M. Intrator and Megan Scribner (San Francisco: Jossey-Bass, 2007), xxix–xxx.

9. Used with permission from Ashley Abercrombie.

Chapter 9 Reconciled Reconcilers

1. Mike Harvie, Jonathan James, and Sem Schaap, "Nothing Here Is Broken," recorded live at LIFE Worship church in Bradford, England in 2016, copyright © 2016 Integrity Worship Music and Life Worship, CCLI: 7053313.

2. Martin Smith, "Obsession," released by Delirious? on *Live & In the Can* (UK: Furious/Sparrow, 1996).

3. Synonyms, STANDS4 LLC, 2017, s.v. "reconciliation," December 1, 2017, http://www.synonyms.net/antonyms/Reconciliation.

4. Information obtained from Nothing Hidden Ministries, http://nothinghidden.com/. The tool is available on their app found on the menu under "NHM Tools."

Chapter 10 Living toward Eternity

1. Gary Black Jr., *Preparing for Heaven: What Dallas Willard Taught Me about Living, Dying, and Eternal Life* (San Francisco: HarperOne, 2015), 231.

2. A. W. Tozer, *The Pursuit of God* (Harrisburg, PA: Christian Publications, 1948), 1.

3. Brian Simmons, *The Passion Translation: The New Testament with Psalms, Proverbs, and Song of Songs* (Racine, WI: Broadstreet Publishing, 2017), 1118.

4. Tozer, *The Pursuit of God*, xi.

5. Lao-Tzu, also known as Laozi, lived about the fifth century BC and is credited with founding Taoism. This quote is in chapter 64 of his work *Tao Te Ching*.

6. Tozer, *The Pursuit of God*, 2.

7. Ravi Zacharias, Twitter post, November 20, 2013, 5:24 p.m., https://twitter.com/ravizacharias/status/403333034134364161?lang=en.

8. Lewis, *Mere Christianity*, chap. 8.

Andi Andrew has a deep passion to see the fullness of the gospel of Jesus Christ outworked in our everyday lives. Born in Spokane, Washington, and married in Sydney, Australia, she now lives in New York City and is cofounder and copastor of Liberty Church with her husband, Paul. They began Liberty Church in New York City with a heart for cities everywhere, and it now includes local church communities across Manhattan and Brooklyn, as well as St. Petersburg, Florida; San Francisco, California; and Manzini, Swaziland. In 2015, she launched the She Is Free Conference in order to equip and activate women to walk in freedom, strength, and wholeness in spirit, soul, and body. A frequent speaker all over the world and author of *She Is Free: Learning the Truth about the Lies That Hold You Captive*, she and her husband, Paul, live in Brooklyn with their four children, Ezekiel (Zeke), Jesse, Finley, and Samuel.

STAY CONNECTED
WITH THE
AUTHOR

ANDI
ANDREW

ANDIANDREW.COM

FACEBOOK.COM/ANDIANDREW
INSTAGRAM @ANDIANDREW

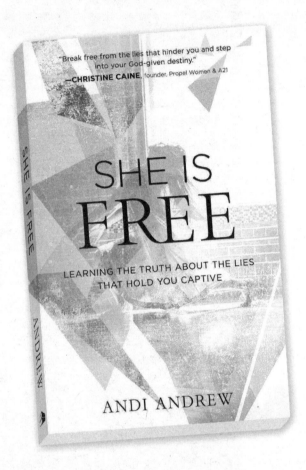

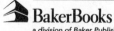

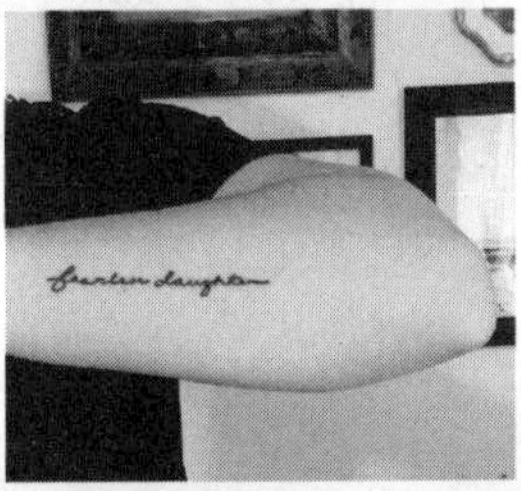

SHE
IS
FREE

BORN

YOU
MATTER